T0194858

THE COMPLICATED LIFE

*Cracking the code on the existence of
life and the way to get back to love*

Reflections, References,
and Revelations

ATHENA PALOMA

BALBOA.PRESS
A DIVISION OF HAY HOUSE

Balboa Press books may be ordered through booksellers or by contacting:

Balboa Press
A Division of Hay House
1663 Liberty Drive
Bloomington, IN 47403
www.balboapress.com
844-682-1282

Interior Graphics/Art Credit: Shayla Hickerson

Print information available on the last page.

ISBN: 978-1-9822-5739-2 (sc)
ISBN: 978-1-9822-5741-5 (hc)
ISBN: 978-1-9822-5740-8 (e)

Library of Congress Control Number: 2020921289

Balboa Press rev. date: 12/03/2020

To my children, who have mirrored the adverse effects of generational trauma
It is through the triggering of the denied pain and suffering that a new choice of liberation was resurrected.

To my husband, who nurtured a genuine paradigm of love
I am eternally grateful.

A DECLARATION

IN EXASPERATION WITH ME AND what I am accomplishing, my youngest son exclaimed, "Mom! You can't go around changing definitions of mental health!"

Why not? I wasn't getting the answers and felt helpless. I needed to lift myself from anxiety and depression. I went out to find a way to get the answers myself. This book will change the norms of the mental health community as it builds up competence in those who have dealt with the 'less than' syndrome (existing less than who you really are, in a reality that is less than what it could be).

I said to my son that I believed he was depressed because of A, B, and C, which he was demonstrating in his attitudes and behaviors. He denied it. He said depression was a mental illness, and he wasn't mentally ill.

I responded, "To depress means to push down or shut down. A person who is depressed has the true self shut down from living. In depression, self is committed to something outside of living, as self is blocked from its own way being visibly important."

And I do believe that most of us are depressed and numb to the effects of how it follows through in personal existence.

I told him to read this book before he started a debate with me on this declaration I have made. He is resistant to knowing more, as he has committed negativity to his existence.

Are you ready to commit competence in positivity as existence? If so, read on.

CONTENTS

Part One: Uncovering Your Truth

Part Two: Realizing the Duality of Our Existence

Part One

Uncovering Your Truth

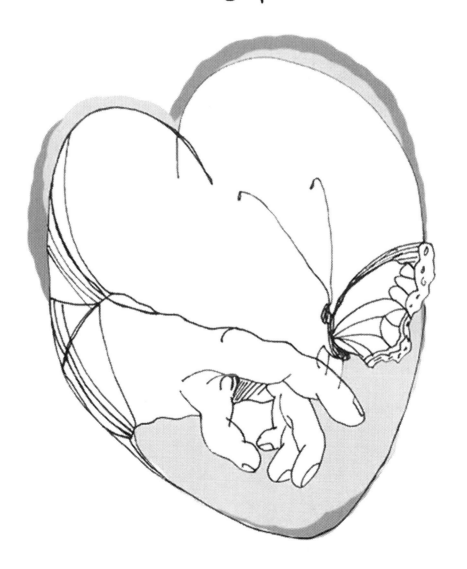

PREFACE

I DID A SURVEY TO see where stress lies for people, and I noticed that no matter how much care people put into their lives, they still end up looking outside of themselves for something more—but most people do not know what that *more* is.

I also asked if they had been diagnosed with a mental illness and, if so, if they had received the support they fully needed to live well. Again, the answer was that they had received support but were searching for more, as they didn't get the relief they needed to live—not only to live well but to the uplifted vision that they held within themselves. People know they are meant to express more but are unsure of what that it is or how to go about doing it in an authentic way that will be accepted and received.

Most stress is tangible and easily recognized: work, intimacy, money, sex, taking care of kids and elderly parents. But the main stress that affects people the most is intangible. You don't easily recognize it, yet it affects every single aspect of you and your relationship to life.

I came to understand humanity—what we might experience as stress, why we do what we do for relief, and why some can heal so quickly while others, such as myself, just can't move beyond our perceived pain, suffering, and struggle. My insights will garner criticism and doubt because I am revealing fresh ways of looking at popular paradigms. As you read, keep an open mind, as it is in resistance that growth stagnates.

We feel alone in our stress, not realizing that most times the people around us are dealing with the same issues. I hope that this resource will offer understanding, hope, and relief.

Moving forward, let us start with an analogy between the journey of the tree and the journey of our own evolution toward well-being.

Consider the Journey of the Tree

The tree's evolution started within the womb of the seed, nourished by the nutrients of the ground beneath.

Over time, the tree sprang through the ground, reaching to the sky's first ray of light. It had a sense of self and knew it was important to move forward in its growth. The roots that grew underneath the soil provided the foundation to its ever-growing sense of self; they varied in width and structure and grew deep and strong.

Over time, the tree imagined itself through the array of branches, leaves, and fruits made possible by its foundation.

What makes the tree flourish or die? The healthiness and sturdiness of its foundation determines its survive-or-thrive state of being.

There is so much under the surface that needs to be acknowledged and attended to, yet it can be hard to understand what it is going through if we do not understand the making of its foundation and what it needs to thrive. We would have to do some research.

The Same for Us

There is so much about us of which we are not aware. Are our current stories those of certainty and security, or are they stories of fear, anxiety, striving, loneliness, and uncertainty?

We can tell by what we are producing in our lives.

In the structure of the tree, depletion starts with the roots. Splitting of personality can happen here—suppress, avoid, self-preserve, adapt.

Moving up to the trunk, it consists of a few main threads that run the course from birth, as we know it, but in actuality, it's before conception to now. It interconnects the mind-set of assumptions, limiting beliefs, intentions, and impacts, with an outcome of conflict, obligation, and ways of being (my life doesn't make a difference, as I am a burden).

The branches support the threads through control, escape patterns, disapproval, idealization, focus (what you pay attention to), undoing, dissociation, and characteristics of associations

The leaves: the expression of "my way" is limited through feeling exasperated in expressing yourself, overwhelm, envy, debilitating convictions, and inappropriate associations.

The fruits: existing is about following through with acting like a burden by constricted self-importance, abuse of love, assuming the worst, and exasperated isolation of innocence.

Just as we would have to learn how to bring a weakened tree back to its inherent health and well-being, so too do we need to learn how to bring ourselves back to health, well-being, and the actualization of our potential.

This becomes an extensive journey back to the self, as there is so much under the surface to uncover and above the surface of which we are not yet aware. It takes time to acknowledge how the nonserving effects of yesterday influence our current way of living. It takes waking up and becoming aware to access the inner models of relating and self-perpetuating cycles stored within.

Sometimes, the answer you seek is right in front of your eyes, but most times the answer needs to be dug up, released of its imbalances, and lovingly restored to its inherent value.

For long-term success, it takes patience and effort to learn how to embody tendencies (an inclination toward a particular characteristic or type of behavior) that will dictate your essence's purpose.

I invite you to take this time today to invest in the evolution of the intention of essence. You were created to experience living by engaging in this intimate development of this venture called life; thus, you are invited to align with the forgotten, forbidden, suppressed parts of you to become fully you and fully alive!

Have patience with yourself. This is a space where no judgments are allowed. Suspend any that might come along.

If emotion arises, allow it to run its course, blow your nose, and begin again.

Take these words and apply them, as if a friend were talking to you with care and recognition for what you have experienced and for the person that you truly are.

Don't take these words as only my words. What do they trigger in you? What experience is trying to arise from reading these reflections? There is something in here for you, yet it might not jump out at you. If you become resistant, zoned out, angry, or judgmental, know that you are being triggered. If something doesn't make sense, take notes and pass over it; keep on going. This is meant for everyone, but not everyone is ready to understand or accept the information and work with it. And that is okay. Let us start.

1

WISE CORE TECHNIQUE

I NEED TO INTRODUCE YOU to a technique I created that has supported me in my quest to recover myself. As I haven't yet opened up the part of the mind that holds my memories in confidence, I haven't been able to access my childhood to consciously discern what it is that influences me to struggle, hide, detach, and zone out of my life.

I call the technique Wise Core Consulting, as everything I need to know about myself, as well as every answer I seek, is stored within. It is a matter of consulting with my energy that makes it quite a challenge, as it isn't a skill that is readily learned and acquired; I am learning as I go. The technique brings me on a philosophical journey into the realms of my deepest stored wisdom of the subconscious mind, body meanings, and inherited scars.

Through the technique's written format, I can uncover the answers to all the questions that pertain to human evolution through *muscle-testing* inquiries, as I have come to realize my interconnectedness with my Creator.

Muscle testing: when the mind holds a stressful thought, an electrical conflict is created in the brain that sends a signal of weakness through the body. A conflict between the conscious and the subconscious results in a weakened muscle response that indicates an answer of *no*; if there is a positive connection to the inquiry, then the muscle response comes up as a *yes*. I muscle test the words until a yes comes up.

Wise Core Consulting is a fresh paradigm (model) of relating that fills in the missing pieces to not only my own but the mental health field's understanding of what liberation entails. Ninety percent of this book uses the technique for clarity, understanding, clearing, and balancing.

The technique comprises individual words. From my body, pulling up the first word, I would inquire into the next word until I could intuitively form a sentence that makes sense to me. Then I would go to the next layer of the sentence forming until I got to the core of the issue.

It takes time and care; I look up most words in my Merriam-Webster's pocket dictionary or Wikipedia's online dictionary to make sure I have the most appropriate meaning, as there usually are more than one to draw on. And sometimes, I have to add to the meaning, as there hasn't been enough information to fully explain higher knowing.

Wise Core Consulting

- uncovers the "meat" of the issue,
- reveals the adverse effects,
- reveals the impact and the consequences,
- is the way to break free, and
- is the way to restore.

My journal posts are titled "Self-Inquiry" when I use wise core consulting to gain more clarity, more substance, and the truth.

This story evolves. What came up for me in the moment is what I wrote down on paper. I have intertwined my inquiries with the collective's experience, as I strongly believe we are all connected by energy—what causes me to suffer causes someone else to suffer too.

When I work with people, I get triggered. And when people come to me for help, but I don't have an answer, it gets me inquiring. I have encountered enough people in my life to see that most of us struggle with the same core issues, even though they may present themselves a little differently, so out of my personal learning, pay attention to what jumps out at you.

Caution: You can get triggered. But know that the trigger will pass. Sit with it and quietly journal what needs to come up. Keep yourself open to the possibilities of learning something new and releasing that with which you didn't realize you were struggling. You have the power within to delve deep and come out securely on the other side.

The soul communicates at a much higher level of vibration than the human mind can communicate, and it comes across as such. I have tried to normalize the communication, but restructuring meanings is not my natural skill as of yet. If what you read seems complex and complicated, skip over it. But be aware that the mind can resist your understanding the material. Be patient with yourself.

This journey took a lot of energy, focus, and faith to get through it. I hope that what has been uncovered will be of comfort and lead to your understanding what might cause you pain, sorrow, or disconnection. We are interconnected, and when God speaks to me, God is speaking to all of us.

Following is an example of what came up for me in the beginning, when I was trying to piece together the missing pieces of the puzzle—the puzzle being my life's struggle to just live.

I will start with uncovering the dysfunctional cord between Grandma, Mom, and me.

My mom said a few times in my childhood that until Grandma died, we would never be close. Grandma died, but Mom and I don't talk. This triangle enforced great disparity to abide by as my own reality.

Generational Trauma

By what am I governed? I don't feel as though I have control over my life.

Trauma through maternal lineage started with the history of my grandma.

Something painfully traumatic happened to her. She disconnected from her sense of self. It was never talked about. She married and, soon after, discontinued having intimate relations.

Fear set in when her daughter came along, as she believed a big burden would happen if she came out of her individual bubble of protection. She was afraid that her daughter would hurt her. All the indifference others perceived from her was the effect of a split in her personality.

She was not consciously aware of herself or her influence on others. She knew she wasn't adequate as a mother. She believed she had a second chance with the birth of her child's first child, a daughter (me).

The effects of the trauma on Grandma: stagnant to self-imagine as she rationalized that she was the guilty party. She limited positive influence as she was considered a nobody. Her state of being was "I am unwanted." Play small; stay invisible.

The effects on her daughter, who is my mom: Her mom was envious of her, giving her the impression that she was a mistake. My mom was undecided about her mom's feelings toward her. She disabled self-imagining (structuring a mental picture of self), as she was emotionally neglected. She repressed her mom's indifference toward her and rationalized that she was the guilty party. Her mom disapproved of the fantasy world in which her daughter lived. My mom expected her mom to ruin her efforts that contributed to the unfolding of her personal life.

She held a sense of "therapy"—that something was seriously wrong with her. She carried the weight of a disability of not being good enough. She felt if she lifted that weight, she would disintegrate into nothingness; the weight held her together. She enforced resistance to anyone lifting the weight, as loved ones would flee when they saw nothing. She became codependent on receiving love, care, and validation from others.

The effects on her granddaughter, who is me: I have been left holding the energy of the post-trauma of my mom's neglect. I hold a sense of therapy and a mind-set of insignificance. I repress, which constricts to self-imagining. I hold a low value of self and believe I bring a bigger burden to everyone's life. I am exasperated at not being seen or heard. I hold Mom's influences of "I'm bad; I'm a mistake; I'm too stupid; I'm nothing" and split in personality.

I repress all sense of self, as it has been my duty to carry the weight of the family's inequities. I definitely am not to outshine my family. It is the bond of making sure that I am not "being somebody" that keeps me attached to my maternal line.

I need to know how I have passed this on to my children.

The effects on her great-granddaughter, who is my daughter: She represses significance. She holds a belief of "I'm a mistake who brings a bigger burden" and a mental pattern of holding low value of self. She copes by living in a fantasy world. She is indifferent in her approach to life, yet she is always producing life. She has learned to flee from self; this shows up as anxious thoughts.

She envies the imagining of others and fantasizes living their lives. She believes, "I'm inadequate to hold high value for self, as I am the burden in life." A part of her holds back from identifying with being value to others.

My influence on the relationship with my sons: I am not enough as a mother. I hold an emotional tendency to be suspicious of their love toward me. I undo paying attention to encouraging love as Mom's envy denies individual specialness.

I fear outshining my mom's relationship with her boys, as I am only good for carrying her burden of "I am a mistake at love." I am inadequate to repress this burden, as I am nothing at being somebody. My boys get anxious-attaching from me.

Through the maternal lineage influence, what connects us all?

- Low self-value
- Belief that "I am a mistake, and I bring a bigger burden to others and self."
- Being discouraged to self-imagine assuming the best of self
- Lack of self-esteem
- Beliefs of "I'm a nobody; I'm a mistake; I'm unlovable; I'm not special"
- Being inadequate to self-imagine importance for self
- Dissociating from being good enough
- Dissociating from receiving good
- Comparing, blaming, and criticizing ourselves
- Inability to trust others
- Craving yet avoiding intimacy
- Overthinking and over-striving
- Questioning our value in relationships
- Needing constant validation
- Having trouble expressing emotions, as well as personality

As you can see, there are no labels mentioned here, only attributes of generational shutdown to the real self.

Let's move on, as there is a lot to uncover. Life is like an onion, with many layers to peel.

Following are reflections on the many aspects of what life encompasses.

2

EMOTIONAL ENERGY

EMOTIONAL ENERGY CULTIVATES IN YOUR body as the absorption of other people's emotions, instincts, intuition, personal perspectives, assuming the best of, and protection against imbalances.

As we live distracted in our minds, the emotional body keeps tabs on whatever brings us out of alignment with well-being. The emotional body aligns with attaching to the energy of our stress, to progress being aware of how we attune with pain, struggle, and suffering.

Positive energy is harnessed within you by compassion, courage, forgiveness, and faith and is gathered from your outer world by supportive friends, creative work, laughter, and movement. Imagine yourself as having an internal pitcher; when it is filled with positive emotional energy, you feel energized about your life—hopeful, positive, charitable, caring, patient, focused, and loving.

Negative energy depletes your pitcher and keeps you small and unhealthy; it alienates you from your best self. Your emotional energy is depleted when there is continuous criticism, abuse, fear, self-loathing, rage, or shame. You will find yourself feeling inadequate, tired, critical, bitter, withholding, and hopeless.

Depending on what is going on in your life, the amount of emotional energy you have in your "pitcher" will vary. Just as physical energy comes from physical self-care, such as exercise, diet, and rest, emotional energy comes from emotional self-care, such as prayer, living a life that makes you feel inspired, hopefulness, self-confidence, creativity, playfulness, and passion.

Emotional energy is drained when you constantly give to others at the expense of yourself, when you are in an abusive relationship, or when you disconnect from your authentic self.

In the beginning, your emotional energy is cultivated through your childhood experiences. If you grow up with positive energy, then you will feel a lightness going into your adult life. If you grow up with negative energy, you will feel heavy and sad going into adulthood. In any given moment, you can change your emotional energy. Adults have the capacity to make a conscious choice; it takes action and willingness to change it.

Some people confuse being depressed with being emotionally worn out. Is your emotional-energy tank full or empty? When you start to feel really good about yourself and your life, do you sabotage it, possibly by getting involved with people and activities that drain you?

Pay attention to your emotional state and how you behave toward it.

Are you consistent in a self-care regimen? If not, start now. Watch your thoughts. Get deeper with your breathing. Engage in an activity. Say hi to someone new. Give a compliment to yourself and then to someone else.

What are you paying attention to?

3

THE COMMUNICATION
OF YOUR BODY

I HAVE TO COME TO believe that we consist of the *brain* (visible and tangible), which is the central processing unit of the body and plays a key role in translating the content of the *mind* (the invisible and transcendent world of thoughts, feelings, attitudes, beliefs, memories, and imagination) into complex patterns of nerve-cell firing and chemical release. The brain is the physical organ most associated with mind and consciousness, but the mind is not confined to the brain. The intelligence of your mind permeates every cell of your body, not just brain cells. Your mind has tremendous power over all bodily systems.*

The mind/body holds an emotional reference of everything we hold true about us. We do not have to remember anything; just tap into our energy by muscle testing and/or mindful journaling and we can access a lot of the answers we seek.

Unprocessed emotions, limiting beliefs, and ways of being all reside in your mind and try to communicate to you through

> discomfort (something doesn't sit right with you),
> pain (physical, psychological, and emotional), and/or
> behavior (ways of being that do not serve you).

Trauma drama is the continuous cycle of pain and discomfort you experience as the result of the effects of unidentified trauma. Most of us unknowingly have been traumatized, and our daily stressors are the outcomes of that trauma drama.

Your stressors of today have been dictated by the trauma drama of

---

* B. William Salt II, MD, "What Is the Difference between the Mind and the Brain?" sharecare.com.

➢ the suppression of emotions;

➢ the influences of codependence;

➢ mind-set and emotional tendencies that can keep you trapped in self-perpetuating cycles of pain, negative behaviors, and sabotaging attitudes;

➢ the influences of power struggle, regret, hurt, sabotage, abuse, neglect, or heartbreak, which will hold you back from happiness, purpose, significance, value, self-expression, and assurance; and

➢ dissociating from subjectivity (inner world). You tirelessly work at trying to survive the injustice of objectivity's (outer world) projection of not being good enough.

These are the steps the body goes through to enable balancing of its emotional body.[†]

Whisper, Yell, Two-by-Four

Your body never lies. Becoming aware of its whispers is the quickest, most direct route to bringing yourself back into balance. Through focused breathing, you can cultivate the sensitivity to become aware and perceive within yourself the whispers your body gives to you.

Your emotions, limiting beliefs, emotional tendencies, and mind-sets underlie the whispers your body is expressing. What is it trying to express? Consider the first signs of stress or imbalance as the *whisper*.

Examples of a *whisper* are

➢ heart beating faster;

➢ shallow breathing or holding your breath;

➢ belly tightening;

➢ clenching jaw and/or grinding your teeth at night;

➢ tightening or tensing your neck or any part of the body.

If you have learned to suppress your emotions, thus being unable to identify and relieve the whisper, your body upgrades to the *yell*.

[†] http://www.healthandwellnesscoaching.org.

Examples of a *yell* are

➤ headache, body aches;
➤ upset stomach;
➤ cranky, depressed mood;
➤ fatigue and/or brain fog.

If you disregard the yell, the body tries to get your attention again; this time, you get hit with a *two-by-four*.

Examples of *two-by-four* are

➤ disease, illness, diagnosis;
➤ injury or accidents;
➤ making big mistakes;
➤ resorting to violence;
➤ divorce or breakup.

Whether stress is physical, emotional, or mental, where there is a limitation, restriction, or blockage, there is a body communication (meaning) to decode.

Sometimes, a yell comes about seemingly out of the blue. Why?

As you stop and take a break, your body becomes relaxed. A pain or discomfort occurs as a signal that you need to attend to something, usually a way of being that hasn't served you but you've stayed attached to it.

When you come back after a time away, you can get triggered into old patterns that you haven't become aware of yet. This is telling you that it is time to acknowledge them to come into balance.

If you aren't taking responsibility for something, the body tries to connect you with the truth.

Nothing comes your way by chance! You are not a victim of circumstance!

There is an explanation for *everything* that you experience. From the animals that cross your path, repeated numbers that you see, the attitudes you receive from others, the pains in your body, sickness, disease, diagnosis, feeling stuck, lost, or defeated—it all is trying to wake you up and get your attention.

An example—a red fox crossed my path.

Self-inquiry: it represents that I need to see something more clearly. The effect of objectivity (the power of others) and the injustice of being treated like a burden is a power loss for me. The objectivity of inferiority caused me never to realize my special purpose. This held me back from associating with a concept that I have been working toward—coming into my power to be. I became disconnected from associating my gifts and talents with my power to be. I compartmentalized them as I scattered my sense of self.

Your life exhibits suffering for a few reasons. Because the mind has successfully denied the trauma drama, the body tries to self-regulate its value by revealing the underlying patterns of objectivity.

The essence of self intends to communicate something that is not directly expressed, called a *meaning.*

Meanings

- Meaning 1: It arises out of consciousness—your desire to be more aware and awake. How have you defined yourself (positively or negatively, subjectively or objectively)?
- Meaning 2: It encourages abandoning self-judgments, which brings about a fresh understanding. How do you self-regulate (govern your own way without outside assistance or influence; subjective vs objective)?
- Meaning 3: It releases depression held toward personal acknowledgment. How are you held back or down? How do you take yourself for granted, especially when things are good? It restores contributing to assuming the best of self being subjectively aligned with personal reality.

The subconscious cycles of pain look like undesirable attitudes and behaviors of the following:

Internalizing: mind-sets and emotional tendencies of depression, overthinking, critical thinking, discouragement

Externalizing: reactions of anger, resentment, judgment, disapproval, playing safe

Symptomizing: bringing on uncomfortable and painful physical symptoms in the body because it is futile to subjectively reveal the underlying patterns

Anesthetizing: self-soothing your sense of not being good enough through substances (food, drugs, wine), activities (shop, gossip, gambling, overworking, overcompensating, overdoing), or self-sabotage.

Where do you see yourself in these cycles? Are you in denial or just not aware?

The Body

Why does the system (physical, mental, emotional) fall into a degenerative backslide over the years? We know that aging is a small part of it, but what else can it be?

It is self-denial that leads to neglect of self-care.

How true are you living to an authentic expression of self?

Before we move forward into the story of your life, let's understand what or who God is, as I have referenced this concept quite a bit.

4

WHO ARE YOU IN GOD?

"HOW CAN I TRUST IN a god if I can't even trust myself or trust others? And how could there be a god out there, loving me, when all I have experienced is pain and struggle? My experiences say that there is no God."

There are reasons why you might not trust in something that you can't see. Start with what you brought into this life from the womb. You absorb the energy of your mother's nutrients that feed her—from her diet to her thoughts, beliefs, assumptions, emotions, and influences of the sperm. Add in your experiences, influences of others, and nurturing in the first few years of life.

> ➢ Did you get a sense that you are more than what you could perceive with your senses?
> ➢ Did you get a sense that you are a part of a bigger, loving, encouraging, duo-knowing entity?
> ➢ Did you learn that you are all alone in this fight called life?

This Is Who I Am

Through all of your experiences, influences, and decisions, your mind has built a structure (consisting of your childhood views) to identify who you are. Out of this identification, you filter incoming information so that it fits with life, as your environment defines it; then you react to life, based on these filters by which you guide yourself. Do these filters arise from a *lower attunement* of the five senses that relate to the physical world or from a *higher attunement* that connects to the spiritual realm?

Most often the lower attunement is afraid to connect with the higher one—to become whole in its existence—as it holds a mind-set of futility and emotions of inadequacy that arise from maturing love as a validation that it is an imposter. This mind-set and emotions bring about indecisiveness about connecting to self-imagining importance; it expects to receive disapproval, so it disables knowing complete.

The lower self is a divisible force that discourages alignment with the higher self.

The conflict is inadequacy in contributing to self-imagining importance, as it discourages value for self. You learned that it's not okay to overwhelm someone else's struggle to define his or her sense of self, so you hold back from holding value for yourself. This is a learned way of being. What is underneath this energy is *blame* through other parties. They blame themselves for the injustices they survived. For them, it's easier to focus on you lacking than on their feeling of being overwhelmed, so they project inadequacy onto you. You learned to take this on as a personal quality.

The way of being of assuming the worst in you and others keeps you disconnected from your essence and always has you searching outward for the answer that lies inward.

Assuming the Worst of You

Constricting importance has you assume the worst of yourself, as it controls how safe you feel in empowering allowable room for a definite way of self-importance. This means that to feel safe comes from feeling equal. If you don't feel equal, your existence is in question. If you lack authority over your way, then you will be susceptible to constricting self-importance, which leads to assuming the worst in you and others, due to a lack of respect for your reality and from being considered unequal from lacking value.

What does interconnection of the lower and higher self look like?

The Layers of the Lower Self
Me of blame
Me of regret
Me of denial

Me of judgment
Me of exasperation
Me of not being good enough
Me of assuming the worst
Me of being a bigger burden
Me of anticipating pacifying discouragement
Me of insignificance
Me of "something is wrong with me"
Me of fear to outshine another
Me at being passive at recognizing envy
Me of not being satisfied with my efforts

The Layers of the Higher Self
Me of self-love
Me of being good enough
Me of stagnating objectivity to be in tune with subjectivity
Me of encouraging self-imagining
Me of connecting to self-defining
Me of contributing to self-assurance
Me of valuing myself
Me of self-importance
Me of being competent in self-imagining
Me of trusting my knowing
Me of being complete
Me of assuming the best of me
Me playing big
Me feeling safe in belonging

A New Awareness

The 'big bang' is the culmination of the energy of love (light side of God) and love validated an imposter or a lie (the dark side of God) being brought to the light of visibility.

In this light of visibility, the interconnection of essence with how you portray the self (structure of the physical self), integrates with either the "lower consciousness," arising from the physical, emotional, and mental structuring, or the "upper consciousness," empowered by essence which is competent in imagination, instinct, intuition, truth and love. Essence is unlimited in love and eternal in life, interconnected to the right spirit of Beloved or the light side of God, known as the Holy Spirit.

Holy Spirit wants to create and experience through each of us, living in a physical, human reality. But if we tend to relate only to the physical realm and deny this curious collaboration, not only do we disconnect to the wonder of who we are and can be in the larger picture of life but we are headstrong instead of heart competent in connecting with life of others and nature.

To note, there are two spirits of God: the dark spirit of negativity which matures love as the imposter or lie; and the light spirit of positivity that matures love as competent in governing self as complete.

The light spirit of positivity is the provider energy of the universe. Does your self respond as being the receiver of this spirit's commitment to heart competence being visible in the energy of positivity? Or, validated an imposter, has your self over extended competence with being less than a portrayal of truth because self believes it will be recognized in judgment (imposter or lie) which keeps you at the frequency of maturing essence as invisible (fed through the dark spirit of God). You are the frequency when you attune with being complete. And complete is "positivity's competence in ruling essence the light of living."

Knowing complete interconnects with the energy of light, represented as "the liberation to which essence is committed."

It gives us an honest sense of being or existence. Disconnect from essence, and you lose upper consciousness (being awake and aware) of inspiration, information, purpose, intuition, truth, trust, and karma, which all come from positivity's competence that commits to interconnecting presence with the Holy team).

Through this disconnection, Holy Spirit steers the lower consciousness into contributing to life's unfolding. This can play out as very confident in mental health but constricted in heart health. It can also play out as you receiving abundance of prosperity (money) yet lack heart attunement with essence. You can find yourself participating in life but with less competence interconnecting presence with self-complete.

Light and Dark

We are all born of both sides of God- the dark and light, negativity and positivity; what has our being been interconnected to? Our cells are the energy of the boundary that we have interconnected with- positivity or negativity. Most of us are constricted by the dark boundary due to the follow through of being imprinted with scarcity. Scarcity is the shut-down of superiority mothering complete.

The role of the Holy team (Holy Spirit, Jesus, angels) is to be the keeper of complete.

The essence of me moves forward and this invisible force adds a twist of scarcity that blindsides me from perceiving me complete in superiority (being true to me.) I never experienced the satisfaction of a job well done. There is always pain and discomfort in everything I do.

In positivity, the team interconnects their essence with ours to support regulating subjectivity as the mind of living; but in negativity, the team has to contend with the "dark force."

The Dark Force

The intention of the D.F. is to interconnect presence with negativity to deactivate and take down positivity's competence to over-ride the bullying of the dark force.

The dark force takes hold of the mind of scarcity and commits it to distressing essence when interconnecting presence with superiority (being true to self).

There is something strong in presence that needs to come up but the D.F. is resisting it. I will keep going, knowing that it will eventually show itself.

5

LOVE

WHAT IS LOVE?

It starts with family. Love establishes family as a focus of internalizing a state of being there for each other, uplifted into a paradigm of importance in being true to self.

Love stands apart from scarcity to assume an influence that organically empowers the value of self and others.

At the core, love is about reinforcing complete as one's existence.

Love expresses as an act of being important and having significance, which creates an outcome of mini-expressions established as love, such as tucking your baby into bed, writing a love song, cooking a celebratory meal, or blowing a kiss. It's the energy that is being there for someone; being accountable; being sincere in its attention.

Love is complete. Everything outside of love has an attachment to scarcity (either a strong one or a weak one).

Becoming

When the egg and the sperm join together, if the process of becoming is undermined, the embryo self-destructs in belonging to its environment, as there is no security of love of self being okay to nurture. This is a denial of being love. In denial, there is futility in recognizing the self as being authentic as love because love is recognized as a lie or imposter in its existence.

"What is happening? What am I doing wrong? How am I wrong for living? I shouldn't have been born! I will never matter."

If you did not feel safe in the womb, you will be anxious about attaching to the outside world, as you will be helpless to trust that you can assume the best of you and what is to come. An energy worker told me that I resisted leaving the womb, as I was certain that life was against me.

A power struggle to assume the best of the self comes into play—anxious attaching (lower self) vs. reinforcing assuming the best of being complete (higher self). Another power struggle comes into play when entering the world and interconnecting self with the energy that is prominent in focus (negativity or positivity).

There is another aspect to consider: when the egg and the sperm meet, hereditary attachments influence the developing self. Are these influences positive or negative in nature?

Energies of attunement: Both the lower and higher energies are equal in focus, with attending to attaching to the self as existence. But by what is the self influenced? Is the influence strongest in the higher attunement of the "truth being superiority" (more on this coming up), or is it influenced to live in the "distortions of lower attunement of inferiority and playing small?"

If primal focuses more on the energies of the lower frequencies (negativity), the child becomes shut down from attaching to the higher frequency of positivity.

Love

The lower frequency's ideation of love is a paradigm of inferiority.

What triggers inferiority? It is the influence to cause one to assume less of self.

The higher frequency's ideation of love is a paradigm of existing as complete.

In adulthood, I have brought deprivation forth, viewing others as ungiving and uncaring.

A lot of women feel insignificant in contributing to family and society; thus, the Me Too movement is essentially trying to balance the inequality women face on a daily basis. Men need to see women as being of value for there to be any chance of women being considered equal. And women need to see men as partners in equality so they can allow support from them to flow. Abuse and discrimination cannot happen in love. But we need to realize that this assumption that women are not treated fairly or equally comes from our childhood paradigm of relating with each other. This hurt sense of self can have us acting toxic in our relations. We can become anxious, fearful, dissociative, or dismissive when it comes to being honest in expressing ourselves. This has us avoidant where it concerns being vulnerable in showing up and trusting others with showing ourselves and getting our needs met.

Equality of importance starts with humanity of self as a whole. Not until we can each see ourselves as being whole, valuable and complete in love, will we be able to view each other in the same way. When we feel low about ourselves, it is part of the human conditioning to keep others around us low, as we feel we are in the company of likeness. In fear, we hold each other back, or we hold each other down.

Enough! If you are a part of this problem, that makes you a part of the solution.

Start by noticing how you are treating yourself today.

6

WHAT DOES JESUS DO?

JESUS COMMITTED HIMSELF TO EXISTENCE as love.

He encourages positivity to exert security in the presence of love by interconnecting with the presence that redirects negativity away from causing love suffering.

We can be competent in love and positivity and still fall short of knowing self as complete.

We control how we interconnect presence with truth; portraying competence in normal is being in-tune with self-love. Normal is validating love (self) an expression of appropriate when alienating temperament from negativity. For a lot of us, we unknowingly mature normal as a lie; the lie is that normal isn't true love.

Jesus exists to bring up trauma drama so we may align with his energy that expresses complete while tenderly establishing control over "pained." Jesus interconnects his presence with my mind to reinforce the mind's biochemical shift of restoring and strengthening.

Look to Jesus for a playout of what *complete* reinforces as.

Jesus is the truth of what assertive satisfaction in being true to soul looks like, in which he is a positive influence through our passive-aggressive disapproval of attuning with self-importance.

How are most people passive-aggressive in life's stress while only a few are assertive in rising above it?

We are *passive* by settling into it. We are *aggressive* in identifying with it. We are *assertive* in disappointing the acting out of self-approval.

Assertive is branded as disappointing—it is disappointing that we assertively pay attention to connecting individuality with significance, as others would prefer to see us suffering than have themselves suffer. And it is disappointing that we prevent ourselves from moving up and forward into our own lives, as how dare we think we are all that. We are damned if we do live to our highest potential and damned if we don't.

Jesus knows his importance in God as Beloved, and he experiences satisfaction in attuning with Beloved.

God's essence of *positivity* is expressed in a paradigm of living. Feminine and masculine energy is not of God but are a living diagnosis of superiority when assuming wholeness. Superiority attunes to living by way of assuming the best of one's value. One's value assumes respective establishing of superiority.

Jesus has a specific role in our lives—one of validating living as subjective, as Jesus knows living apart from suffering.

The power of the Crucifixion is a focus on superiority interconnecting essence with the security of one's faith in establishing the light side of God as presence.

Evolving Jesus

Higher knowing—did negativity of existing seep in when the positivity of the big bang of consciousness came into living? Yes. And we all have a connection with negativity, right? Yes. But most attune to it, while others can dismiss its influence. Is Jesus God incarnated? Yes. Am I? Yes, as we are all born from the same consciousness. Is it the same in context? No. How is it not? (1) Jesus has no tie to negativity, and (2) Jesus was born through the light of God (no earthly conception) to encourage, through demonstration, the truth of that love.

Next question: how does Jesus call God Father? God is not the pronoun *he*, but he is referenced as Father. Father means "committed to positivity, light and love." Jesus assumes God to be loving in God's commitment to realize Jesus as an imagining of greatness. Jesus is dependent on God for guidance but was not meant to be dependent on God for aligning with him in persecution, as light of God does not establish superiority with persecution.

What does the cross of persecution represent? It represents the power to restore through the playout of competence by the team of Jesus, Holy Spirit and angels.

God wants Jesus to be an influence of service, not servitude to the people of "suicidal" (preserving the shutdown to love). Jesus impacts empowered living by his subjective example of superiority. Jesus died for his attachment to assuming the best of living, empowered by the divine attunement, with his follow-through to governing the light of love as the human way to be.

Most of us exist; only a few truly live.

Superiority is the theme, so let's go into that.

SUPERIORITY

SUPERIORITY IS THE WAY OF the truth of positivity. Superiority is the innate knowing; innate learning style; individual skill set; sincere, honest, sensitive, compassionate, positive, optimistic sense of self.

The paradigm of superiority is validating positivity as the source (the play out) that expresses love. It looks like this:

- Taking personal responsibility
- Pride in effort
- Self-value
- Self-importance
- Commitment to personal authenticity
- Projection of assuming the best of self
- Manifesting in flow
- Trusting
- Loving
- Open–mindedness; open heart
- Sincerity
- Attuned to truth of self

In nurturing superiority, the feminine is sensitive; quick to detect or respond to slight changes, signals, or influences, and assumes the best of helping to restore personal insecurities.

The masculine is assertive attachment, assumes the best of the feminine contributing, and protects the vulnerability of that attachment.

Together, they align to attach to a paradigm of superiority, existing as a reality of being equal in value and interconnected as one.

Let's go deeper into this thread.

Superiority of the Female

For a lot of us, restoring superiority moves us away from doing anything about being constricted in our existence as we choose to reinforce the masculine value and energy. I believe we reinforce for a few reasons:

1. The feminine energy, as well as one's own truth, has been denied existence.
2. The influence of the masculine has been overpowering in personal conditioning of equality.
3. Depriving nurture deprives the heart from sufficiently developing.
4. Girls are taught to assume the best of attaching to the males' modeling of importance before their own. Around the world, most girls' importance is not even a consideration.

We commit ourselves as good women, and behind every great man is a good woman, upholding his importance. And there is nothing wrong in this reinforcement of the masculine energy and value, until it has us shift away from influencing an assumption that, in being female, we are important, powerful, significant, and valued in our own accord.

The hurting of feminine superiority can restrict a male's follow-through with restoring a female's importance if the male is committed to negativity which discourages the positivity of feminine independence. A lot of people are not aware that they have been committed to negativity as a reality to abide by; thus, it makes it difficult to enforce a change with underlying resistance.

Women are superior when they assume the best of their guidance, with tuning in with the privilege of empowering the male's influence to provide by nurturing their efforts. The feminine energy nurtures, supports, soothes, and encourages the masculine energy of focus, determination, and follow-through of provision. Remember that a woman has both the masculine and feminine energy as equal in essence. In regarding the masculine and feminine energy as equal, a woman can employ either energy in any given situation and receive the same amount of value as a male would in doing the same thing.

The importance of women aligning with equality has become about assuming the best of self-value by focusing on influencing an association with assertive self-approval and with assertive self-interest. This would be considered the feminist movement, but in asserting self-interest, the woman denies empowering the man to "imprint," assuming the best of supporting the woman in her progress.

The man needs the woman, and the woman needs the man to influence the power to be real in value.

There are women of the movement that employ principles that they detest in men. They have unknowingly become more bitter in their stance that they don't need men, not realizing that the feminine energy has competence in independence.

Superiority of the Male

Men are contributors of value. They value women as equal partners in the collaboration of life, and they value women's efforts to support them in their efforts to provide—what? There is a block. I'll try again. Men contribute to value by constricting a woman's right to tune in with her value. (This is my interpretation. Is it yours too?)

We know what the woman does for the man, but what does the man do for the woman?

The man shifts away from following through with bringing the woman forward in equality.

This rings as reality for quite a number of women, but does this make it true?

If I reflect on Jesus's relationship with Martha, the sinful woman, I see he openly allowed the persecuted to wash his feet, dry them with her hair, and rub them with expensive perfume. He tuned in to her support, and by doing so, he elevated her value. Knowing he thinks of her as being equal encourages her to assume the best to bring herself forward in appraising superiority/self, as Jesus aligned with her follow-through of positivity.

I recently noticed the impact that my husband's significance has had on my life. Without it, I wouldn't be doing what I am currently doing. Actually, he has supported me from the day I met him; I just couldn't see that past my insecurities of a man's focus.

Do I support him in return? Yes, but I do not see it.

I do not see the significance of my impacting being seen as competent in value (in who I am and what I can contribute), as my love hasn't made a visible difference thus far.

Self-inquiry: empowering superiority tunes in with resisting the male's love for his beloved.

I get it, as I have experienced it through the transcendence from boyfriends to marriage.

I did not learn what love from a male would do for the security of knowing me as complete in being a woman. I have been cheated on more than once. I did not see myself as important or equal to them. I did not see what I offered to them as value. I did not see *me* in the relationship. I was zoned out from making sure that my lover fully participated in the follow-through of love when I showed up in positivity. But then, I couldn't tell if I was loving or not.

When I am insecure, I cannot see my husband for who he really is, and I cannot trust his efforts in putting himself forth in support of me. When I am good with me, I am open to receiving from him, which lights him up. My support comes from accepting his provision to take care of me, and it also comes from accepting me as I am and following through with bringing me forward in my fullness.

My husband is not insecure in my personal development. He is not trying to keep me close to home. He trusts me. He loves me. His openness allowed me to start trusting again.

Equality has nothing to do with physical size or strength, intelligence, power, resources, religion, politics, or capability. Equality is the right to employ positivity of importance as ones' existence, valued just as important as the next person's.

8

SELF-IMPORTANCE

YOU WOULD LIKE TO LIVE a happy, healthy, and fulfilling life, yet have you been able to achieve it? Honestly? Keep reading, as a lot of us believe we are living such a life, but—

You want to be encouraged to grow into your best self through imagining a self-concept that outshines any insecurity, yet you play small, hidden from living out your best life. You want to be secure in a loving relationship, satisfied in a job that provides a good income while valuing your efforts, and relaxed in your leisure time, yet you seem to face so much suffering, striving, failures, and disappointments throughout your day. Broken relationships, job dissatisfaction, money problems, health diagnosis—many experience joylessness and incompleteness in their daily existences.

How is it that you can feel so comfortable in your struggles yet so unhappy or detached when you seem to have everything?

The answer lies in what cannot be seen.

And what is it?

It is a lack of value for self-importance, which looks like personal indifference, envy for the lives of others when they succeed, hopelessness within the world's chaos, depression with life as we currently experience it, anxiety of the unknown, and resentment of failed opportunities.

When I ask people what self-importance means, they think it is being selfish.

If you google *self-importance*, you'll likely see definitions like "narcissism" and "thinking too highly of yourself."

If you google *importance*, you'll find "a state or fact of being of great significance or value."

This is a neutral paradigm of relating to importance, but why does attaching importance to the self add a negative connotation to it? It signifies being a mistake if you were to hold importance for the self.

So if you cannot assume the best—viewing yourself as important—then no wonder life breaks down. No wonder you become depressed and anxiety over what can happen stops any follow-through of bringing the self forward successfully. You *cannot* value something or someone that is not considered important.

Definition of *importance*: agreeing to attune to one's reality to empower self-value.

Importance represents an empowering of one's subjective reality.

Description of *importance*: fitting in; following through; empowering; assuming the best of; valuing; significance; and approval when the real you shows up.

Definition of *value*: (1) the regard that something or someone is held to deserve; the importance, worth, or usefulness of something or someone; (2) a person's principles or standards of behavior; one's reality of what is considered value.

Importance is the inner, soft voice, "balance of locus of control," which is of mind, body, spirit, and soul.

Importance focuses on nurturing appraisal of self-assurance; assurance is found in the interconnected importance of the whole self.

What is "narcissism and thinking too highly of yourself" if it isn't self-importance?

It represents congested (blocked) importance. You haven't aligned with the truth of your significance, as you gave your power away—as a child, you were a victim of this disempowerment, as there were no boundaries set to indicate what was right and what was wrong. As an adult, you have the power to take back autonomy of establishing boundaries for a reality of subjectivity (internal locus of control).

A lot of people have been led to believe that fear causes stress in their lives, but most times, it is anxiousness. We experience worry, unease, or nervousness when we demonstrate competence in being true to ourselves due to negativity's influence, dictating how we should be.

It is time to understand how you got to where you are so you can expect to receive something new for yourself.

You can have the happy, fulfilled life you desire; it starts with taking personal responsibility to work toward something different from the comfort, reliability, and focus of that which you already know. I admit that it is easy to subscribe but hard to follow through with it.

In the Beginning

Is baby valued or not?

A baby's communication is made through movement and nonverbal sounds. As a baby you conveyed your wants and needs by crying, flailing your arms and legs, smiling, cooing, and snuggling. If the caregiver took the time to understand your signals and then responded with appropriate nurture, you felt safe and secure and formed an attachment to loving support.

These nonverbal forms of information (tone of voice, touch, smell, facial expressions, body posture) become the emotional backdrop on which you will build your self-imagining of importance, which consists of beliefs, points of view, prejudices, expectations, assumptions, and imaginings about how life is going to be or how you are going to be in the form of energy (outcomes).

You can only appropriately imagine yourself if you interconnect the essence of you with positivity. Negativity validates interconnecting essence with life as existing, whereas interconnecting essence with positivity constitutes living, not just existing or surviving. And in living, there is self-importance, while in existing, there is judgment.

The Missing Paradigm Shift

Assume the best of how you want to contribute to self-importance, instead of yielding to the guidance of others who reside in judgment.

A lot of us were not nurtured to follow through in developing self-imagining, as we were conditioned to live by someone else's rules, loyalties, duties, and expectations that didn't include the truth of us in surviving.

Were you celebrated for your everyday living, or do you only remember being yelled at for something but never were sure what for? Was moodiness or helplessness the energy of love?

I have talked to people who were traumatized by foster care or boarding school. This environment of putting yourself last and serving the power above was often the "nurturing" that broke the young child's self-imagining of importance. If this is your primary source of infliction, then have that be your umbrella of what scars the rest of your life's story.

Either way, through parenting, boarding school, adoption, fostering, or another form of primal mode, we were discouraged from being individually aligned within. But I am referencing attuning with birth parents, moving forward.

Primal mode is the primitive, primary, or fundamental way or manner of identifying and nurturing the individual and the bonding of each person in family as unique in what is brought to the relationship.

Did you, as this child, experience enough display of love, security, and appreciation to form a strong attachment of trust, or did you experience more anxiety, rigidity, criticism, and fear to form an emotional background of distrust and uncertainty and an attachment of inferiority? With distrust and insecurity comes assuming the worst of self, and others, as you haven't measured up to their standards of being good enough to fit in and belong. Where is God in all this? How many of us were taught that we had a higher self to attune to so we could be in tune with positivity redirecting negativity?

If you experienced emotional disconnect, injury, trauma, or being committed to scarcity, you would grow up and form a distorted view of who you are and what you can expect to receive from this world. This view and emotional backdrop that you have acquired follows you everywhere; every decision made arises from this emotional backdrop. This view is how you will perceive your everyday world, and you will only take in information that fits within this internal view. You get from life what you unconsciously expect to receive through your view, and you react to life based on the decision you made about this view. If your fundamental need for love is met, you will form a view that your world is a safe and consistent place, in which you assume the best of self, others, nature, and God.

Everything you understand revolves around your internal revelations and view, which began to form from your mother's womb, through her influencing your atmosphere, and continues to contribute to the function of your emotional backdrop. If you associate a parent's disapproval with insecurity, you will internalize it and believe that there is something wrong with you—that you are not good enough—as it is all about you in your own mind—this all happens on the conscious level of the lower self.

Moving forward, you would make decisions to perceive of yourself and behave in a certain way. You learn to forego parts of yourself (dissociate) to take care of your parents' or caregivers' well-being and hold/carry/own/ take responsibility for their energy in the form of

- loyalties (strong feeling of support or allegiance),
- patterns (give a regular or intelligible form to a way of being),
- duty (moral or legal obligation; a responsibility to keep life happening a certain way),
- imprints (come to recognize self in a certain way),
- pacts (formal agreements),
- contracts (agreements intended to be enforced),
- promises (assurance that you will do, live, act, and be a certain way),
- parallel living (living that is similar to another),
- limitations and restrictions,
- influences (the capacity to have an effect on the character, development, or behavior of someone),
- beliefs/mind-sets (the established set of attitudes held by someone), and
- discourse (an established way of being).

Children often learn to take sides and support one parent over the other. This leaves children being adamant that one parent deserves their love, support, approval, and encouragement over the other. And they rationalize that the parents' inequities can be excused.

Why would children keep reassuring their parents' perfectionism, while ignoring any neglect they might have suffered?

If children believe that they aren't enough and that they bring a bigger burden to a parent's life, they set out to prove their adequacy and resist holding self-importance so that their parent will be okay.

They don't understand the underlying deception to which they have been made to adhere. The children's right to self-imagine and hold importance was squashed as they preserve that lie to be relevant and to be the truth.

They hold a clear *no* to having self-respect as duty takes over. Duty associates with care of someone else before self. This is a learned response.

This response is detrimental to the developing of self's imagining of importance. Moving forward, the effects can be damaging.

The Effects of Being Unimportant

- ➢ Defensive
- ➢ Believe "I am a mistake"
- ➢ Discouraged
- ➢ Believe "I have nothing to offer"
- ➢ Can't outshine discouragement
- ➢ Angry with feeling insignificant
- ➢ Jealous of seeing the significance in others
- ➢ Indecisiveness and second-guessing
- ➢ Take responsibility for stuff that isn't mine
- ➢ Feel like I am a burden, and I bring the burden to the lives of others
- ➢ Avoid encouraging efficacy to self-imagining wholeness
- ➢ Unwilling to acknowledge appeasing someone else's well-being
- ➢ Dissociate from abandoning the role of playing small

Do you struggle with remembering your past? A forgotten past indicates underlying trauma.

As children cannot digest adult drama, they will disconnect if they feel or perceive being unloved, unwanted, uncared for, and mistreated.

Those who bounce back easier don't have a fundamental way of being that states, "People assume the worst of me in perceiving me incomplete."

And this is the other part of the missing piece: self-importance can only be nurtured if you know you exist and are complete in that existence.

The Effects of Feeling Incomplete

- • Having a variety of health issues
- • Mental health diagnosis

- Inferiority—looking for approval, apologizing for everything, taking responsibility for stuff that isn't of you, loneliness, power struggles, inner conflict, not measuring up, not being good enough, negativity, pessimism, over-striving, perfectionism
- Constricting importance—not standing up for yourself, denying yourself contribution, downplaying your achievements
- Congested reality—playing small, not being noticed, excusing yourself
- Damaged importance—depression, overcompensating, lost self; lack of self-satisfaction
- Pretending to be something you're not (feeling like a fake)
- Overcompensating—take measures to attempt to correct or make amends for a perceived personal error, weakness, or problem to fit in and belong. You give up on being true to you so that you can fit in and belong to what you perceive has more value for you (their way over your way). You become the caregiver or go the other way and try to wear too many hats.
- Feeling overcome—helplessness, overwhelmed, sabotage

Giving in to their way over your way damages self-importance, and you think that others assume the worst of you and your way.

I have seen the constricted importance of the leaders in the school system, politics, religion, and coaching. This is how I see it projected:

➢ Let's be friends—there is a lack of boundaries between the two people.
➢ I am the teacher—patronizing attitude of knowing best.
➢ I am the superior—you need me; I don't need you.
➢ In competition—envy seeks out gaining one up.
➢ Caretake, people-please, overcompensate, selfless—this support suffocates or smothers
➢ What's in it for me? How can I get my needs met?

When we feel out of control and helpless with our stress, we usually try to dump our experience of being overwhelmed onto someone else, as it feels too heavy to carry for ourselves.

In reality, most people do not realize that their minds are hurt, and thus, they don't do anything about it. Or if they do something about it, it usually involves taking medication.

Medication does not cure the hurt or damaged mind but for most, until they can figure out what exactly is stressing them out, medication can bring security to the energy of helplessness.

9

OBJECTIVITY VS. SUBJECTIVITY

HAVE YOU LEARNED TO DISSOCIATE yourself from your own inner knowing to live by the rules of others? Do you guide your life subjectively or objectively?

Subjectivity derives from an individual viewpoint, bias, mind-set, how you feel about self and life, a state of being good enough, special purpose, anticipation of satisfaction, undoing of envy, and denying disappointment and disapproval to have it affect you. You live true to you, as you know your existence is of value.

Objectivity exists outside of your thoughts and feelings. Objectivity projects envy, disapproval, resentment, and perfectionism. Your response to objectivity is indecisiveness, displacement (you find something repressing or unacceptable, so you manipulate, substitute, or influence it for something more acceptable), feeling you are a mistake, and dissociating (removing or separating yourself) from subjectivity, thus emotionally disconnecting. You live as an extension of someone or something else which makes subjectivity disempowered.

Inquiry

By age eight, a substantial mind-set can form. The mind-set is based on a context of objectivity—one of less real/more real. Subjectivity denies being aware of the encouragement to be significant, as objectivity has you believe it's futile to be aware of encouragement, as you are not special. ("If only I was adequate at being good enough at being real.") You feel misguided with regard to subjectivity and special purpose, as you are led by objectivity.

Around age fourteen, a possible mental health diagnosis consists of a mind-set that it's futile to be smart enough and to grasp that objectivity stagnates being good enough. You lose your power to be. You feel misled with regard to the injustice of being the bigger liability.

To some degree, we all have a fear of punishment from others (judgment, discredit, teasing, criticism) so we are cautious about what we share of ourselves.

This is living objectively, as we gave in to the possibility of receiving punishment instead of subjectively realizing our value within and walking with our heads held high with self-esteem.

Often, we manipulate the mask we wear to control our environment.

If a stage in personal development is shut down and prevented from developing, then the child cannot move forward to expecting full attunement with self. Narcissism is at the core of being shut down.

Being shut down means that the child has a *clear no* (no allowance) to acknowledging and developing any part of self; thus, the child is not allowed to progress with subjectivity as a mind-set of sovereignty.

A Note on Narcissism

I am talking about people's selfish intentions toward you. They don't see you as a person, so they treat you as unequal and inferior. They look at you suspiciously. They hold resentment toward you and your decisions. They lack nurturing anything good about you, as they are jealous of your good. They make you question yourself and doubt your ability to come into your own sense of self. Essentially, they suck the energy out of you and render you dependent on them. They project love and care for you by doing for you, but they do not have that capability. They are codependent, keeping you small and tied to them so that you do not have the power to leave. They believe they will fall apart if you "abandon" them. Everything seems rosy, as they make you feel alive, but you are only alive to them to the degree that you fill their empty love tanks within. They need you to show them loyalty by putting them first as your focus.

It is when you take yourself out of that relationship that you can see the effects, not before, as you are entwined in the lies and the loyalty you hold to them.

If you have a narcissistic person to this degree in your life—for you to be friends, a lover, their child, or their parent—you need to view yourself as an equal. Understand that the lack of value they hold toward you has nothing to do with you, personally. They are hurting bad within, as they have been emotionally abandoned, abused, and neglected; it is not your responsibility to heal them.

Do not protect them. Do not appease them. They will look at your behavior with suspicion and a lack of trust. This will have you forever trying to prove yourself good enough to them. Be aware of the "Disney parent"—one who seems so involved with spending money on the child, showing the child a good time, acting like the higher figure with grand intentions—because underneath that façade is the adult's anxiousness in attaching, to an assumption that their child's importance is equal to their own. In anxiousness, the adult constricts the importance of the child's reality being approved of as it's not the adult's reality of what value entails. As long as the child provides to the adult what the adult needs to feel alive, all is fun and friendly.

Narcissism shuts you down from identifying with the energy of engaging in love, as it is satisfied in the undoing of satisfaction found in love's engagement. Narcissism pains identifying with the engaging in love by guilt (blame), punishment (undermining), and penalty (avoidance of being lovestruck).

Lovestruck is engaging in an individual desire to embrace the significance of being in love and being loved, by always evolving, being assertive in being fully satisfied with being important in love, and creating loving connections through that energy.

In narcissism, you need to abide by the narcissists' rules if you want to have relationships with them. Restore your value, and then set your boundaries against their control. If they cannot handle it, then you will have to cut the connection. But the power of value lies with you. See yourself as having value so that you do not seek it through them.

It is so sad when children have to forget who they are so that their own parents can exist.

Most people do not realize that they are objectively driven. I am sure that any of our stress is due to being objectively focused. It can be stress in a relationship, at work, with well-being, money, sex, or self-expression. We give of our time, attention, and resources, but we often do not get back in equal consideration. I don't mean you should keep tabs to make sure that you get back in the same amount as you give, but if people are taking advantage of you or if you are not considered equal in value, they will demand that you prove or earn your keep to be considered worthy by them. Do not fall into that trap. Stand guard for self-importance to take center stage in your life.

10

MENTAL HEALTH (SUICIDE)

MENTAL HEALTH IS A MIND-SET that interconnects

➤ personal experience/existence,
➤ a definitive, clear *yes* to personal security for one's way,
➤ encouragement of "my way," and
➤ assuming the best of your engagement with belonging and creating space to allow setting focus on your reality and its existence, for an outcome of self-approval toward self-value.

Suicidal: to hold a mind-set that would turn against one's autonomy; it is an inherited imbalance, distortion, limitation, resistance, or damage that informs the shame of not being good enough. It is a trauma of giving the impression that people have no right to hold self-value, which makes them feel less real, which represents being broken. They would forgo pride and believe that they bring a bigger burden to life, as their inner sense of inferiority makes them unconsciously act like a hidden danger.

The consequence is that they will internalize this belief that they are not good enough and appease the familial (systemic) abuse by taking ownership of the family's pride (systemic guilt), to be great over their own sense of completeness. They take it on as they perceive that it is their place to carry the weight of the trauma.

A belief that forms is, "I am inferior to the nurturing of being good enough, as I need to earn validation." And this has them striving to prove their worthiness, moving forward.

They are not aware of this holding of duty to the trauma, as they have been disconnected from integrating a clear yes to holding self-significance. Inferiority has become a natural way of being.

Through a gradual sinking of significance, they have learned to distrust and hold indifference for self.

Suicidal is a shutdown from realizing self-potential and value, as self doesn't have a mind-set of complete. In this paradigm, there is no hope or solution available to bring self out of the paradigm of helplessness, and it is suicidal to think or do otherwise.

What needs to be done? Relinquish objectivity's (other people's) guiding that sabotages an influence of subjectivity (personal reasoning), by following through with assuming the best of personal existing. (I know there is more to add to this but it's taking it's time to come up for me.)

There is a woman who is global with her business of helping young people, but when I see her, I don't see the joy that it would bring, coming from her. She seems flat to me, and even though she smiles, there is no approval of what she has done in her smile or body language.

I think about popular social media personalities who have committed suicide, and I can relate to the lack of joy that I saw in their eyes and the way they held themselves.

I realize the next layer that comes from the exasperation of helplessness that encompasses the mind is the struggle with holding pride for our efforts, as we never learned to identify positively with the self-satisfaction of being real, as we were never nurtured into attuning with our true selves. We fight holding approval for ourselves, which turns into indifference for our accomplishments.

Do you feel like a phony, and are you worried about being discovered as one?

Do you allow only so much goodness in?

Do you only accept certain parts of yourself as good enough?

Do you limit self-satisfaction?

Do you expect others to disapprove of your self-expression?

Do you have friends but feel hollow in the intimacy of maintaining them?

This comes from a false sense of self—a part of you that believes it is fake. But we feel fake because we were not nurtured, guided, focused on, or encouraged to feel real and whole.

As for me and the same for you—my dear, there is nothing fake about you. Self-importance can never be taken away. You are always of value. It is time to reclaim that denied and judged part of you. You are whole, just as you are.

I need to share a viewpoint regarding personal pain.

I remember reading that the mass killings by guns in the United States are not the result of mental illnesses and that only 3–4 percent of mental illness diagnoses actually hurt people.

What? How can one quantify that statement?

Someone once shared his pain history with me. He said, "Athena, I was in so much physical pain, and when the bully of the boss started digging into me, I could vividly see exactly how I was going to rip his eyes out. Don't ask me how I did not do it.'

Pain can cause injury.

Pain can cause death.

Pain causes dissociation from self.

One doesn't need to be diagnosed with mental illness to be able to hurt someone else.

Most people could be diagnosed with some label under the umbrella of mental illness and not even know it.

A Side Note on Suicide

I used to believe that we all have the power to take control over the governing of our own lives, but my own journey into the depths of despair has me realizing that shutdown does not allow attuning with one's right to restore existence.

Let's move on to identifying trauma and its effects.

11

TRAUMA

WIKIPEDIA.COM DEFINES *PSYCHOLOGICAL OR EMOTIONAL trauma* as a type of damage or injury to the mind that occurs as a result of a severely distressing event and that may result in challenges in functioning or coping normally after the event. While emotional trauma is a normal response to a disturbing event, it becomes post-traumatic stress disorder (PTSD) when your nervous system gets "stuck," and you remain in psychological shock, unable to make sense of what happened or to process your emotions.

Everyone has experienced trauma, as it is part of the human experience.

Trauma can be situational, in that it occurs one time. You can get hurt from a broken heart from a breakup of a relationship. You can lose a job, lose a child, or lose a mortgage on your house. You can experience trauma from a hurtful comment, a grade D, or being kicked out of a club. Some have gone to war and have experienced the aftermath of death, destruction, and disempowerment. Some have endured horrific sights and circumstances in their field of work.

Wikipedia states that vicarious trauma is the emotional residue of exposure that counselors experience from working with people's trauma stories and becoming witnesses to the pain, fear, and terror that the traumatized have endured.

Vicarious traumatization (VT) is a transformation in the self that results from empathic engagement with traumatized clients and their reports of traumatic experiences. Its hallmark is disrupted spirituality or a disruption in the trauma workers' perceived meaning and hope.

Trauma from consistency (reinforcing a debilitating mind-set as being normal) often aggravates the futility of getting over it and moving on.

I have come to define the trauma of psychological abuse (also referred to as psychological violence, emotional abuse, or mental abuse) as characterized by someone's subjecting or exposing you to behavior, attitudes, influences, or manipulation and the objective experience that may result in psychological trauma, including inequality and a contributing to a reality of nonexistence or post-traumatic stress disorder, including constricting importance and disempowering valuing self-importance.

The trauma of *emotional neglect* is a failure to notice, attend to, or to respond appropriately to children's feelings or developing of their self-imagining self-importance. Because it's an act of omission, it's not visible, noticeable, memorable, or sufficient in regard to the emotional needs of the child. It is subtle yet harmful, as it is overlooked as it does its silent damage to your life.

As an adult, it leaves you questioning yourself and others and damages how you want to empower the reality of your existence.

It has you

- doubt yourself,
- hide and shut down to your authenticity,
- struggle with self-discipline,
- struggle with follow-through,
- not understand your feelings or another person's feelings,
- close off to your emotions,
- not trust or rely on others or yourself, and
- feel incomplete.

It makes you feel disconnected to yourself, as you were denied the support and encouragement to develop imagining self-importance in the forming of your life.

If you cannot face the facts of trauma as separate from yourself and release yourself from the emotional impact, then you are still struggling with the aftermath of the trauma.

The thing is, unless you have been diagnosed with PTSD, you won't necessarily recognize that you are affected by trauma, as trauma can be silent, expected, and thought of as trivial and easily put to the side, never to be thought of again. Most do not know that their struggles can be traced back to a certain event or cycle of pain, and they find it hard to pinpoint the cause of their trauma.

Trauma is anything for which you cannot find a resolution, that disconnects or separates you, that objectifies you in some way, or has you envious, which has you believe you are incomplete.

Most struggles, insecurities, discomfort, bodily pain, disease, undesirable behavior, and cycles of pain and discouragement are effects of trauma.

When the trauma gets triggered, you react—from being overwhelmed through the flight/fight/freeze response.

It is a mind-set of, "It's inadequate to resent the contribution trauma makes because it projects me as being a mistake for being discouraged by the trauma."

The idea is that you need to "Man up! Don't be a sissy! Don't be selfish!"

You internalize the trauma to represent something about you; you do not want to acknowledge the mind-set of injustice that it entails, as it triggers inequality. You are taught to handle your inner struggle with positive thoughts and distraction to get your mind away from being overwhelmed, but that just bandages the open wound; it does not clean the infection and close the wound. Don't think that you will recognize this being overwhelmed as a loud and obnoxious emotion because, most times, it is hidden from your consciousness.

🦋 🦋 🦋

You can carry the influence of trauma without experiencing it. It can be inherited from one generation to the next.

Trauma can be passed down through the following:

- Inherited DNA (limitations, imbalances, congestion and distortions)
- Influences (abuse, neglect, distortions)
- Circumstances (a death, abuse, divorce, bullying)
- Emotional pain points (emotional body)
- Short and long circuits in the brain
- A power loss of spirit (disconnection; lack a power to be)
- Disability (not being able to move emotionally and physically; mind-set of being broken and awkward)

- State of being not worthy of experiencing significance
- Reversal (acting in an opposite way that is nonserving)
- High-functioning trauma that leads to haughtiness (the appearance or quality of being arrogantly superior and disdainful)
- Pretending, leading to behavior (speaking and acting so as to make it appear that something is the case when, in fact, it is not)
- Drama (a continuing series of events or circumstances)
- Imprints

Trauma induces a belief of, "I am a mistake, and I bring a bigger burden to life," which encourages unconscious living, which often leads to behavioral disorders.

Being a bigger burden represents "states of shame."

An example of the effects of trauma is forgoing identifying with a self-concept because of the trauma of being "less real."

Being "less real" means that you were not nurtured to be subjectively complete.

Effects of Being Less Real

- Losing power to be
- Feeling undervalued
- Feeling blamed
- Feeling resented
- Forgoing subjectivity
- Denying disapproval toward the self

12

THE INFLUENCES
THAT GUIDE YOU

INFLUENCE IS THE CAPACITY TO have an effect on the character, development, or behavior of someone or something or the effect itself.

As a child, you accepted—voluntarily and without reluctance—your familial influence over your self-imagining (structuring a mental picture of self).

You learned to look toward your parents or caregivers to guide, teach, support and encourage you to become the best version of yourself. You trusted that they knew best and would give you sound advice. You listened to them and heeded their advice and discipline. You wanted to please them and willingly did things to gain their approval, which, in turn, fed your sense of significance. Their presence influenced your image—the person you saw yourself becoming.

What happens when a parent/caregiver isn't there to nurture with support, encouragement, and direction in the development of an individualized sense of self?

Physically, the parent was there—to go to work, pay the bills, clean the house, feed you, and get you to bed—but emotionally, the parent was too tired, unavailable, distant, abusive, or impassive toward what you were doing and who you were becoming. You might have felt ignored and not important enough to gain attention, or you might have over-strived to become a version that your parent wanted you to be or that you believed you needed to be.

In either scenario the foundation is set. You know what to expect for yourself moving forward and you living according to it.

If you learned to trust that your emotional needs would be met, you would move forward, trusting your own decisions. You would know that you are good enough, and you would praise yourself for a job well done. You would also experience life as people assuming the best of you, so you would easily follow through with putting yourself out there and drawing people, resources, and experiences to you. You would know you are provided for. You would perceive yourself to be worthy. You would have faith that all is supported. You could relax in pride with the outcome of your success.

Some of us instinctively knew that we were not being treated fairly. We did not learn to trust or hold others and ourselves in high regard. Abuse instilled a framework of self-sacrifice, and we learned to hold our exasperation in silence.

If you learned to distrust and hold indifference for yourself, you would expect that you had to

- depend on yourself,
- not ask for help,
- lack empathy for yourself,
- blame yourself and others,
- take the focus off yourself,
- doubt your accomplishments,
- feel insecure in your relationships,
- get into emotionally unbalanced relationships,
- assume the worst of yourself and of others,
- always strive, never being able to relax in pride for a job well done, and
- lack locus of control and inner boundaries.

Life was either a roller coaster of ups and downs, or life was neutral, and you felt that depression set in quite often. You didn't know how you felt in any given moment because you repressed your emotions to keep you safe. But you weren't safe. You gave in to the illusion that you were safe, but you gave up your truth for the reality of the family's truth, which was _____ (fill in the blank of your experience).

You don't feel that you belong, and you feel misunderstood. You perceive yourself as unworthy, and you don't trust easily. And you do not feel safe existing in your reality, as you expect to be persecuted in some way. You live from your head, closed off from the heart of living.

Let me ask you: do you feel equal in your relationships with your children, your lover, or your coworkers? Would you even know what that would look like, whether you did or didn't?

The adverse effects of having self-importance damaged are as follows:

- Prevents self from fitting in
- Misguides assuming the best of self
- Lacks a mind-set of subjectivity
- Lacks equality of feeling safe with purpose
- Shifts away from existing; hides self from others
- Shifts away from follow-through of qualifying (creating space to set value on the importance of essence and its showing up)
- Fixes attention on the assumption that being real is being bad
- Pigeon-holed as inferior

This is where the conflict of assuming the best of self-existence lies. Even though you were victimized as a child, you still impact yourself today with the effects of damaged importance to prove the best of self by disempowering equality, constricting subjectivity, and denying self-value.

Are the effects of your life your fault?

As a child, no! Whether it was given or whether it was taken away, you learned to perceive yourself through the world and its influences around you. You were vulnerable and impressionable and trusted in the knowing and giving of others around you.

You could have started off living with high self-esteem, but with consistent negative behaviors, limiting beliefs, and attitudes thrust upon you, you changed course (were influenced) and learned to hold indifference for yourself instead. Conversely, if you struggled and suffered during your first few years, love, attention, and nurturing can heal and transform your disabled sense of self.

You might have closed down your memory to your childhood, but deep down, you know that your parents/caregivers were not there for you as you needed them to be. Today, you want their approval and validation, and, unknowingly, you strive for it.

Influences are hard to notice and recognize, as they are not seen.

They are invisible energy, and they can cause havoc—or they can build you up.

How do you know if you are still under the influence of someone or something? Answer the following questions:

- ➢ Have you lived your life according to another person's wishes or attitudes? Example: Did you become a lawyer because your dad wanted one in the family? Do you participate in an activity to gain approval from your mom? Do you stay at something because it would please your dad?
- ➢ Do you feel stuck, blocked, restricted, unsupported, or discouraged to follow your own path? Are you unsure of your path?
- ➢ Do you hold indifference toward yourself and your path?
- ➢ Do you speak up for yourself, or do you fall silent and give in?
- ➢ Do you feel uncertain most of the time? Do you constantly question yourself?
- ➢ Are you close to your parents as long as you do what interests them? Do you grab on to the time that they want to spend with you?
- ➢ Do you make decisions based on your parents' advice or your own?
- ➢ Do you lack compassion for yourself?
- ➢ Do you strive at work and limit your play?
- ➢ Do you rationalize your parents' behavior? Do you internalize that you have done something wrong and that leaves you not being good enough?
- ➢ Do you stand up for your parents, and no one can say anything contrary to what you perceive as good about them?
- ➢ Do you pride yourself on not needing anyone?
- ➢ Do you put other people's care before your own?

Know That …

Influences can be transferred, such as holding the influence for a parent and then transferring it to a child, lover, or a friend. You can still be under the influence of a parent, even if he or she is dead.

You can be influenced not only by your family but by people, politics, and circumstances and by your perceptions and emotions surrounding them.

Note: A parasite (someone who sucks your energy) can strongly influence you if you focus on inferiority and responsibility to that person.

How to Release Yourself from Influences

➢ Accept that you are in denial. Become aware of the influence.

➢ Start to recognize whose voice you are listening to with every choice you make.

➢ Breathe deep from your belly. Get in touch with your emotions as you make decisions through the influence of those emotions.

➢ Stop feeling responsible for stress that isn't of you.

➢ Let go of the label "scapegoat."

➢ Restrict encouraging a childhood script of inferiority by empowering self-importance.

Are you in a relationship where you feel belittled, anxious, unheard, unseen, and/or disrespected? Is the impact of it exasperated self-importance? Do you feel your way, your values, and your beliefs are always in conflict with your loved one's reality, and it leaves you feeling exasperated and out of control by dealing with it? You don't feel important in the relationship which has you wondering, *What is the reason of it all?* After you speak up for yourself, do others come back with passive-aggressive attitudes, such as sarcasm, humiliation, indignation, or self-righteousness, and it has you fighting for equality in the relationship?

If so, this is a power struggle for self-importance.

You both want to be accepted for who you are as individuals, with your own realities of what is true for you.

Their attitude mirrors back to you all the inner childhood pains you have not discovered yet, but that ends up projecting unknowingly back to this person. It is a silent influence of an inherited imbalance (actually, a few inherited imbalances) that disrupts the positive regard you both had for each other in the beginning.

As with the narcissistic, you have to step back from power struggles and restore your value. (Narcissism is a power struggle!)

Power Struggles

A power struggle takes hold if one party feels responsible for or is in support of the welfare of the other before self, and the other party in the struggle controls that relationship. When the responsible one realizes that his or her life makes a difference and again assumes the best of himself or herself, the other party will either attack or let go. Such people can only allow space for those who will bow down to them. They can only control their numbness by bringing themselves up, so if they can't do it through controlling you, they will search elsewhere for another party. This is a power struggle for the privilege of assuming the best of oneself and one's efforts.

Another power struggle is to claim personal power as valid over someone else being valid. This can become a competition (friendly or unfriendly) for an intentional regard of importance. Attitude is "look at me; I am important, and you need me." Sometimes, the truth is misconstrued and personal desire goes against self-accountability.

Another power struggle, based on the personal reflection above, is a reinforcement of systemic colonialism of constricted importance. The system, forces onto the people as truth, that self-importance is best when supportive of inequality, which will give a false sense of pride in who you are when you follow the rules of the system (this is brain washing).

This conflict of an internalized, negative message of inferiority dictates how to assume the best of empowered existence. The struggle is in taking back autonomy to dictate self-love as equal and a value, apart from the systems' dictation.

13

ENVY

WHAT IS UNDER THE PARENT'S (caregiver's) behavior or lack of attention that leads to a child feeling less than, not good enough, inadequate, a liability, too privileged, or a mistake?

The answer is resentment arising from envy. Envy represents the undoing (the cause of your ruin or downfall) of self-imagining importance, which happens as the person resents who you identify as being. Envy stops you from dreaming of who you are and who you can create yourself to be.

Parents (caregivers) are indecisive about their sense of significance; thus, they project discouragement on to their children who are coming into an optimistic sense of self. The energy is, "I want what you have, and if I can't have it, then neither can you."

Envy looks like discouragement, belittling remarks, ignoring, manipulation, humiliation, giving a cold shoulder, moodiness, control, and disapproval. Envy says, "You will never be good enough in my books," and it keeps you striving for their approval, even though you don't realize what is going on. It has you identify with the undoing (canceling or reversing the effects or results of self-imagining importance), and it has you expecting that you will never be good enough.

If you try to step out of this story, it will have you doubting, second-guessing, and being indecisive about the truth of who you really are and what you can expect for yourself. Thus, it has you sabotage your efforts to uphold your dreams, your voice, your confidence, and your purpose, as you have learned to assume the worst of yourself.

Envy is about keeping you down so that you do *not* outshine the parent (caregiver). You will hold an imbalance of resentment toward him or her and an imbalance of alignment toward yourself, as you don't know how to take back your power to be; you lost power through the codependent relationship.

Envy isn't found in the family only. Society, on a whole, is envious. The school fits you into a box. Marketing tries to mold your emotions, your body, and your experiences. Artists create something great, and they are criticized for it. For some, it is easier to type out mean comments than it is to figure out why they are not content.

Envy creates a mind-set of not being good enough, which leads to feeling overwhelmed when moving forward, as you believe people assume the worst of you. Recognize the signs of envy so that you can counteract them.

Signs of Envy

- You are not good enough in their eyes.
- You are blamed for their not feeling good enough about themselves.
- You are given the impression you are "less real" than others.
- They assume the worst of you.
- "If only ..."
- You anticipate feeling powerless.
- They ignore your right to shine.
- They restrict your being in tune with self.
- You hold a loyalty to their desire of satisfaction, while denying your own.

Effects of Envy

- You don't feel lovable.
- You take responsibility for their discouragement.
- You do not stand up for yourself.
- You anticipate disapproval.
- You dissociate from connecting to significance.
- You avoid identifying with self-imagining importance.
- You experience loneliness.
- You experience depression of empowering equality.
- You experience the anxiety of shifting away from allowing space to align with importance.

The Outcome

The trauma of feeling inferior would have you lose power to owning your purpose, as you would be busy taking care of others' sense of feeling insignificant.

Pay attention to how you identify with an exasperated zone-out from anticipating envy's disapproval to undo the effects of envy's conviction of *being* disapproved.

The Effects of Envy's Conviction

- Rationalize approval.
- Escape happiness.
- Become a hermit.
- Feel awkward.
- Move away from follow-through.
- Keep proving the self exists.
- Assume the worst of you.

For me, support represented a competition for attention.

How many of us live as though we are in competition with others? "They can't outdo me on a job. They can't receive more than I did. How did they get a raise and I didn't? How did she get that boyfriend when I am prettier? How did he get that girl when I am stronger? I am the one who deserves that money. I should have been picked." The playing out of competition goes on and on.

Competition has us assume the worst of ourselves as well as the other person; distrust comes into play.

The wall to intimacy comes up. This triggers the fight/flight/freeze response. We close up.

We are not here to be in competition for self-value!

Release yourself from the critical mind of envy.

14

EVERYTHING IS ENERGY

ENERGY IS THE ABILITY TO create

- an outcome;
- a different state of being;
- stagnancy;
- contribution.

Energy is movement, and it either creates a benefit or a liability.

Your thoughts and emotions are energy conductors. They are not naturally static. If you restrict the expression of an emotion, you have blocked it from influencing manifestation into something positive. If you block the influence of having a certain thought manifest, it won't happen. You need to be congruent in thought, emotion, and control. (Control your negative energy, as well as the energy of others that is geared toward you. Only take responsibility for yourself.)

Waves of light and sound vibrate at a frequency through the energy field within and around you. There are positive/light tones of energy and there are negative/heavy tones of energy. Positive and negative tones of energy can vibrate at both a high and low frequency, depending on the state of the influence of the idea you intend to convey. Is the state of the influence one of pessimism or optimism?

Remember that an influence has the capacity to have an effect on the character, development, or behavior of someone or something or on the effect itself.

When an emotion or a thought is released, others can pick it up, depending on the strength of their energy fields. As the energy vibrates, it disrupts emotional tendencies positively and negatively. If you block emotions, you will lack the influence to empower your ability to let go of that which doesn't serve you. Emotions affect living in intangible ways, such as forming a belief about self. What you release with your thoughts, you bring about in tangible ways, as the energy field is magnetic and draws to you whatever you focus on.

Outside influences can trip you up without your being consciously aware of it. These influences can be passed down through the contribution of past generations. They can steer outcomes without your knowledge of it.

Energy that is blocked is actually an inherited distortion of a destructive way of being.

How you are influenced is a good indicator of what you will draw into your life. How you perceive the world around you will dictate which outcomes will be displayed. When you feed lies and indifference to yourself, it puts an imbalance in the magnetic field that affects the whole self because you keep getting exposed to ways that say, "I assume the worst of me and people assume the worst of me."

Get clear on the following:

- Whose voice you are listening to
- What is true and what is a lie that you have held to be true
- What you believe about yourself and the world around you
- What you expect to receive
- What you are resistant to let go of and why
- What you are willing to do to assume the best of yourself

To impact situations, processes, or people means to affect them (make a difference to).

To impact in the context of healing means to bring the self down.

To impact is an effect of *learned helplessness*, which, in psychology, is a mental state in which an organism that is forced to bear aversive stimuli or stimuli that are painful or otherwise unpleasant becomes unable or unwilling to avoid subsequent encounters with those stimuli, even if they are "escapable"—presumably because it has learned that it cannot control the situation.

We become attached to the outcome, as we haven't developed a clear yes to sovereignty over our own lives; it becomes a boundary of support for us.

Some people, in the paradigm of their power to be, detach from objectivity's reality to empower sovereignty (a self-governing state of value). But the damage to one's existence lacks the power-to-be paradigm. One would have to restore the attachment of assuming the best of self to gain an existence of subjectivity, equality, and self-value.

What will it take to become certain of being complete?

It will take not reacting to helplessness, as helplessness underlies everything about the lower self that plays out as a certainty of being incomplete.

I need to let go of reacting to anything that is not of love, as all of that stuff is unimportant and irrelevant.

When I look online to see what is happening around the country, I am flabbergasted at what people will do in the name of love. And the point here is that they truly believe they are acting from love, but that love is the lower self's version that is influenced through negativity. Love, through positivity, is certain of being compassionate, as they honestly care about themselves and each other, knowing that all are equal and just as significant. There is no hurt, pain, shutdown, invisibility, assuming the worst, etc., in true love.

True love does not put one's belief, religion, loyalties ahead of another person's right to live free. But there are people that believe that bonding is nurtured by empowering abuse (it was this way in my family). I watched a video online showing a mother and daughter getting into a fist fight. The daughter ended up on top of the mom on the floor, kicking and punching her in the head repeatedly. There were people milling around. No one stepped in or shouted at them to stop; someone actually filmed it to later upload it (this power trip, considered appropriate, happens way too often). I had to stop watching. I read some of the comments that stated disgust for the daughter treating her mom that way. Why did it start in the first place? Why is abuse the way these two use to communicate their power of self? A mother, or father, should never have to lift a fist to teach, communicate, bond, or prove self worthy of being important. No one should be engaging in physical, emotional, psychological, religious, or manipulative abuse against another and then call it love, referred to as "this is the way it is for us."

Sexual Abuse

I have had conversations with young women and have read stories of those who have shared their sexual escapades—and I cringe. How could a woman hold value for herself when she wakes up to her partner fingering her or taking off the condom before he ejaculates, or she gives him a blow job without getting pleasured herself. Too many young men think that it's okay to treat a woman as though she is to be used for their own pleasure and fulfilling of their needs. A lot of men are not even clear on the paradigms they hold true that diminish the value of a woman. And a lot of women are not aware of validating the man's behavior as being okay and even welcoming. How many men take pride in their sexual conquests, while calling a woman a slut for hers?

I had a conversation with a young male on this subject, and his viewpoint was, "Women call each other sluts in jealousy, and only a small percentage of men are no good, but we are attracted to them, so it's our responsibility to move toward the majority of nice guys." He has substance to share. Yet he should become conscious of the lyrics he listens to that degrade women if he wants to be congruent to his words, actions, and accountability.

This subject isn't talked about, and so many men will say that we have moved past the age of sexual harassment and abuse, but this is so untrue.

What is the mind-set that fuels assault and harassment?

"I matter more than you do."

15

THE TRAP OF CODEPENDENCY

CODEPENDENCY, IN BROAD TERMS, REFERS to the dependence on the needs of or control of another. It also often involves placing a lower priority on one's own needs, while being excessively preoccupied with the needs of others.

Codependency can occur in any type of relationship, including family, work, friendship, romantic, peer, or community relationships. Codependency may also be characterized by denial, low self-esteem, excessive compliance, or control patterns.

Codependents Anonymous offers a list of patterns and characteristics as a tool to aid in self-evaluation of codependency.‡

We are all dependent on someone or something, but it's to the extent that we lose ourselves or stop someone from living his or her life that determines if the relationship will be a benefit or a liability to us both.

Depression is a pushing down of coming into your own sense of liberation. The codependency of keeping you down and being obligated to serve the other before yourself limits your sense of power to keep you from standing up for yourself. Given enough time, you will lose your sense of self and become the image of that you were manipulated into being.

The meaning of depression in codependency is to liberate from anticipating powerlessness.

You anticipate feeling powerless when making personal decisions because you learned that you had no right to stand up for yourself and build value in becoming your own person.

You are valuable. And this knowledge of self-value can only come from within.

If you are eager to be good enough in someone else's eyes, your sense

---

‡ Codependents Anonymous International, "Patterns and Characteristics of Codependence," CoDA.org., http://www.coda.org/tools4recovery/patterns-new.htm.

of worthiness comes from how you think that person perceives and values you, rather than how you value yourself. This external validation will carry through to your other relationships; thus, it is best to encourage self-imagining that holds self-significance. You are the only one who can make you perceive good within.

16

ARE YOU PLAYING VICTIM?

WHEN YOU POINT A FINGER at someone else (blaming) and shrug off responsibility for your own stuff, you are not treating yourself with respect and understanding.

If you believe that you can't solve a problem or make a choice because someone else holds the answer, you are in victimhood.

If you think you are owed something of value (e.g., an apology) in order to move forward, you are in victimhood.

When you let your negative thinking take up free room and board in your head and allow it to take over your life, and it leaves you lying in bed, you are playing victim to it.

When life has to be perfect and you feel you need to be perfect and in control, you're in victimhood.

If you don't feel free to express yourself or are unable to consider your wants and needs before giving in to the demands and wishes of others, you're in victimhood.

If you cannot and will not listen to the other party without your defenses rising, you are in victimhood.

The power of choice always lies within.

Choice: Liability or Benefit?

Are you aware that you almost always have a choice? Sometimes, you might not want to accept the consequence of the choice so you transfer your overwhelming feeling onto someone else and blame that person for the consequence that occurred.

Example: Close to your sixteenth birthday, the principal calls in your dad and announces that you are skipping many classes and that you don't do your homework. Your father makes a choice on your behalf and pulls you out of school to get a job. The impact is in how you handle the situation. Will his actions be a benefit for you by your making the most of it? Or will you make his choice a liability and resent him for what he's done, bringing that attitude with you?

The choice is to agree that your actions demanded a consequence, and you chose to accept it, well or not well. Or the choice is that you don't see how you are responsible in this situation, so you resent Dad for making you do something you don't want to do. You move forward in life with disgust for him, and that influences your attitude going into new situations in a negative tone.

Where does the power lie?

Will you make a choice to bring about a consequence of *benefit*— finding humor in a situation; following through; holding reverence for yourself and others—or *liability*—being envious; blaming; repressing your capabilities; feeling exasperation; bargaining; responding in a state of shame?

The choice of how to respond is yours.

Gaining high respect for you increases assurance in your ability to make positive choices. Restricting encouragement judges your choices as being powerless to bring your way into the light. (Have you figured out your way' yet?)

To change the trajectory of where your life is going takes making a conscious choice for yourself—one of benefit or one of liability. From there, you can (and we usually do) make unconscious choices, but if they are positive choices, they will benefit you; if they are negative choices, they will be a liability.

Either way, you are making choices continuously toward the unraveling of your life. Look around you—have your choices served you or not?

POSTPONE THE GUILT TRIP

RESISTANCE IS THE INTERNAL BLOCK that holds you back and keeps you stuck. The basis of all resistance is guilt and shame. Each of us experiences resistance to some degree. If it keeps you from experiencing change, then it's a sign that you need to learn to open up to it so you can work through it.

The higher the emotional response you feel with a certain situation or trigger, the higher the degree of shame. You will notice that your negative emotional response will lessen as you deal with the emotional impact your issue has on your life.

What internal imbalances are keeping you stuck and unable to move forward?

Internal imbalances are injustices that influence assuming the worst of you.

Guilt means you did something that didn't feel right, and your inner compass is letting you know that you stepped out of your point of power. As a result, you consider changing the behavior. Guilt is also associated with feelings of being a burden or causing an inconvenience and extra stress for others. How many times do you say you're sorry to someone in a day? Ongoing guilt keeps you trapped in your own sense of inappropriateness. Guilt forbids holding self-value.

Shame is a painful belief that you are defective as a human being and that you need to pay for your sins (what others deem unfit about you), so it leaves you believing that you are unworthy of being "fixed." Women over-strive to be the perfect wife, mother, and social volunteer, while men find redemption in their work, feeling overburdened by the demands of family and society's pressure to be strong and hide their emotions.

To fully thrive, we need to slowly disrobe from these demands, labels, and expectations and start to demonstrate our vulnerability in order to fully show up.

If you are reluctant to be vulnerable, it's because of underlying beliefs, such as, "I am damaged. I do not matter. No one cares about me. I'm unlovable." You don't want to feel this so you repress and stagnate developing yourself because you can't be vulnerable in putting the real you out there.

Shame is also about being rejected, exposed, feeling like an outsider, and experiencing self-loathing. Shame through the emotional abuse of humiliation—such as sharp anger, name-calling, rejection, setting someone apart as unacceptable, a searing jab at someone's very essence, and excessive criticism—renders us helpless and pushes us to lash out or hide.

You find fault with yourself because you haven't yet learned to find compassion for your own shame, so you turn your anger, self-judgment, or internalized negative messaging inward and project it out. You don't want to feel the pain, so you place the blame elsewhere. Every time you put pressure on yourself—using comments such as "I should," "I have to," "It's expected that I"—the critical parent that you grew up with comes out and shames you, expecting perfectionism in all that you do. You will transfer that perfectionism to others, expecting them to meet your demands and prove that they love you or that you are okay. Every time you make cruel comments, the angry and disapproving parent comes out through you, and you will demand loyalty to your way but expect disloyalty from others.

The feeling of shame is a spiral into darkness, accompanied with an assortment of critical, judgmental thoughts. Being in this state blocks your capability to process and release it. You must meet your deep and very painful feelings with understanding and acceptance in order for compassion to eventually heal this toxic reservoir of accumulated shame.

Shame says, "I did something wrong, and I am wrong for having done it." Shame is about the worth of you as a person. Shame makes you feel flawed and unworthy of being accepted. Shame starts by existing outside your thoughts and feelings (objectivity), as you somehow have integrated a belief that something is wrong within (subjectivity).

You've been in the mind-set that in order to survive, you need to search outside of yourself for love and approval and search for more. You are punishing yourself. You need to give up your attachments (thinking, seeing, feeling a certain way) and dependencies (to receive validation from others) and emotional tendencies (pride, sabotage, overworking, discouragement, self-loathing) to experience your identity as genuinely perfect.

Your level of suffering is equal to the level of resistance that you are unwilling to give up.

This is the truth!

Shame is a lie you have been led to believe. Shame was put onto you by projections of other people's pain and suffering. They didn't want to process, so they transferred their insecurities, self-contempt of blame, and self-loathing to you. If you currently hold a belief that you are a mistake, know that someone reinforced this state of being in you. They made it about you, but it has nothing to do with you! Deep down, they hold the belief that they are a mistake but ask you to own it and heal it for them. You can't possibly do that, even though you try, and thus, you take on being "the mistake of bringing the bigger burden" and blame yourself for any shortcomings to protect the other person. This is an invisible *influence* of a destructive kind. Until you acknowledge and release the shame in your life, you unknowingly will project your pain onto your loved ones too. It becomes a cycle of pain within your life, and it affects the lives of your children.

18

THE THREE TYPES OF RELATIONSHIPS WITH SELF

The Willing

THE WILLING RELATIONSHIP IS FAVORABLY disposed in the mind from birth, meaning there is no repressing of self.

Those who are willing have integrated a clear *yes* (assurance) to imagine the self as important, and they are prompt to act as they encourage being in tune with self and assuming the best within. They are not influenced objectively. Their duty lies in protecting their self-esteem which sits at their core.

The Repressed

The repressed relationship with self is affected by envy. This causes separation or disconnection from the self.

Those who repress the self will hold trapped emotions of disapproval, which causes them to project resentment. They give in to fears of suspicions. They flee from encouragement. They resist acknowledging their significance, and this splits them from their higher selves.

"I'm nothing" sits at their core. This is an inherited program; they have split from positivity and with God. Their focus is external, objective, and of five senses. They struggle moving forward as they have emotionally shut themselves down. They hold a mind-set of victimhood that becomes their state of being.

The Disconnected

The disconnected relationship with self-regard is envied by the repressed, and their sense of significance is taken away by the repressed. They learned to resist significance because of a belief that "I am fundamentally flawed," which sits at their core. They sink into lower self over time because of the conditioning they received.

They are capable of building a life through contribution, as a lot of disconnected people volunteer and become prominent in society, but they are still disconnected from defining and expressing themselves fully. They deny aspects of themselves, as they learned to dissociate from them growing up.

The higher self is still there, with a duty to shift away from paying attention to the reality of others, to measure up to being equal in empowered importance.

The lower self resists self-imagined importance and is dependent on holding pain, due to a duty to either pacify insignificance or encourage significance for the one who encouraged the disconnection because they feel responsible for the other party's pain and suffering. This results in giving but not often getting back.

What relationship do you hold with yourself?

Do not judge it as right or wrong, good or bad, as this is part of the mind-set that needs to be disabled. You are in a relationship with at least one of these or in transition between two relationships. It's close to impossible to know if you are disconnected, as it has become a natural way of being. Most do not realize that they have hurt minds.

A Few Signs That Could Help

- You feel off, as though something isn't quite right.
- You're discouraged.
- You sabotage gain, or you over-strive for gain.
- You compete for attention.
- You keep searching for the perfect way/knowledge/spirituality/focus.

- You pride yourself on your independence.
- You feel like you don't fit in or are invisible and misunderstood.
- Security is your number-one need.
- You are emotionally numb to your truth.
- You strive for a relationship with someone who is dependent on you; there is a lack of a personal boundaries.

Note: The willing can become disconnected through trauma. Willing can be disconnected to a certain quality, not as a whole.

19

LEVELS OF DISCONNECTION IN THE MIND

THE TYPE OF RELATIONSHIP YOU have with yourself, the trauma you previously experienced, and the drama (cycles of pain) that followed will determine how these disconnections will affect you as you move on.

Short circuit: The disconnection is situational in nature, and it causes you to lose your assurance in yourself and in life for a short time, until it is restored. (Examples: You got a D on a paper. Your date broke it off with you. Your child yelled at you. You didn't get the job.) You need to tap back into the tendency to "be good enough" by partaking in positive experiences to boost your sense of value.

Long circuit: The disconnection is situational in nature, and it causes you to carry a stigma (a mark of disgrace) of not being good enough. (Examples: You got fired. You got divorced. You got into an accident. The bank foreclosed on your house. You were bullied. You filed for bankruptcy.) You need to instill a belief of assurance, as you lost faith in your own competence and capability.

State of influence: This disconnection comes from inherited energy (the repressed). The influence is a parasite—someone is feeding off your energy. The question to ask yourself is, "How much control do they have over my sense of self?" You need to outshine the parasite by doing that which you believe will bring about disapproval, envy, resentment, and disappointment from the person you fear or won't outshine.

Reestablishing a relationship with your self: Wake up and become aware. Take responsibility for you and your life. Uncover what you understand to be true for yourself.

Understand how the belief, "I am the bigger burden," affects you.

Realize "I am a mistake" is not yours to own.

Decide you are good enough.

Be faithful to self-imagining (coming into your own sense of self).

Believe you are more than …

Claim a clear *yes* to defining yourself and reconnecting to positivity.

20

THE ROLE OF EMOTIONS

EMOTIONS ARE THE DRIVING FORCE, the power, and the motor of our lives. You make your daily choices based on your emotional state in any given moment. Without feelings and emotions, you would be like a robot, a computer operating a body. Feelings and emotions, your likes and dislikes, give your life meaning. Do you feel happy or unhappy, fulfilled or dissatisfied?

Feelings are a sense of what you may feel in any part of your body. These may be simple body sensations or vibrations, such as hot or cold, pain, tingling, or stiffness. A feeling is the inner-body experience that you have if you can directly feel the energy associated with an emotion. Every emotion has feeling (energy) to it. To what degree (neutral, mellow, strong) is it felt?

Emotions are reactions about someone or something. You can find yourself angry about someone or something, afraid of something, or in love with someone. An emotion is a learned reaction, based on how you interpret your surroundings, the projections of others, and how you are treated.

You experience your emotions strongly when you are sensitive, as you react immediately and directly to your social and physical environment.

Suppression of your emotions starts as an infant, when you are trained not to cry when you are unhappy. It follows you into adulthood, when you judge your emotions as bad. If the emotion is labeled *bad*, then you assume that you are bad for feeling that emotion, so you shut down to feeling.

You start to view the world as being unsafe and believe that you are alone in your struggle to find peace and happiness. When you start to age, your emotions and feelings greatly diminish because you have learned, over time, to protect yourself from getting hurt. If you don't know what you are feeling at any given time, then you don't learn how to manage your emotions when they arise.

Self-dysregulation (a mismanaging of emotions) arises when you do the following:

- Disintegrate self-significance
- Believe you are being a bigger burden to someone's life
- Suppress your emotions
- Disapprove
- Discourage
- Hold a disability ("Something is wrong with me")
- Betray yourself
- Become diagnosed with a disorder (settle for being a disability)
- Lack nurturing
- Hold a negative representation (e.g., being powerless represents self-imagining)

If you mismanage your emotions, you will be suspicious, which leads to feeling unsure of what to expect or trust from others and second-guessing your own decisions and actions.

Most problems are a result of certain negative emotions (anger, sadness, guilt, embarrassment, blame) that you have attached to experiences along your journey into adulthood. The experience itself is neutral; a problem arises when you assign negative meaning to it through emotion. Then you form beliefs and tendencies as a response to the emotions you feel, and then you believe those emotions that arise from these unconscious ways of being. For example, a friend doesn't put the toilet seat down. You get angry and think he doesn't listen. You unconsciously believe that he doesn't care about you, and you start getting angrier, feeling hurt even more so. The next time he leaves the toilet set up, you automatically go to shame—that you are not worthy enough to be cared about.

The way you feel in any moment reflects to you how you think about yourself and your life. Emotions underlie every choice, decision, and belief you demonstrate for yourself. Whichever emotion is attached to a present experience is generally a result of your perspective, which you derive from your past experience. What you "see" depends on what filters are operating in your life. Your filters color your personal interpretation of the data you receive from the world around you.

These filters gradually build up, together with your life experiences, an accumulation of knowledge and a system of references, associations, and representations. The filters create an unconscious prejudice that goes unnoticed in your overall view of the world. Filters evolve considerably during the first few years of life and stabilize as you reach adulthood.

Filters are the influences of how you are trained to behave—what to believe or not believe; what's acceptable or not acceptable; what is bad or good, beautiful or ugly, right or wrong, black or white.

This is how you learned as a child:

You either instilled a system of conscious personal management of the guiding of your own thoughts, behaviors, and feelings to regulate your behavior (subjective), or you did the opposite and learned to govern yourself through the assistance and influence of the outside world (objective).

Attention becomes the main goal. The search for love and approval begins if you believe that you are a mistake in some way. It's the search for more, and it can only be found "somewhere, out there." Thinking that there's not enough of whatever you're searching for mirrors the belief that you are not enough. The search for happiness keeps you looking outside of yourself. You start accumulating material things, knowledge, and labels to fill the void. Or you make rules, demanding that your expectations be met, for you to feel loved.

To see the world as it really is—with a subjective view—the filters should be recognized and then removed. Becoming favorably inclined in mind is of utmost importance, and this takes time, attention, and effort.

Think back to your first failed relationship. Did it tear a piece of trust away, leaving you vulnerable in the heart? This experience often causes the next relationship to close down before the heart gets hurt again. By walking into a relationship with your guard up, you automatically believe that hurt is around the corner, and that, in the end, opens you up to loneliness and pain because you have shut yourself down to the emotional connection of intimacy.

More and more your life becomes robotic, with compulsive emotional tendencies (acting out, envy, suspicious) and self-absorbing habits (compensating, fantasizing, being disgusted). This leaves you living only in your head, separated from your body and life source of the heart.

Emotions can provide you with the greatest pleasures in life but also with the greatest suffering. You do not want to suffer, so you intentionally diminish your feelings in order to diminish the amount of emotional pain that you think you will feel. Closing down, however, also reduces the amount of pleasure that you can experience. By reducing the suffering that you think you might feel, you also reduce your feelings in your body and will be unable to be in tune with how it is trying to communicate to you. Your vitality and enjoyment of life are weakened. Your increased susceptibility to chronic degenerative disease is a result of the body's cells hanging on to unprocessed emotions (considered the *emotional body*, in which the emotional backdrop is laid). That's a high price to pay for reducing the suffering that you think you might feel by expressing your emotions.

You must understand that you could experience intense suffering for a short term and deal with it, instead of agreeing to low-key, long-term suffering, in which more of your life and body could be affected.

You need to realize that as soon as you acknowledge the emotion, you can tame it, but as long as you ignore it, it silently grows and settles inside your body, distributing havoc on you and your life.

The goal is not to show your vulnerability of the heart and body because, in our culture, that shows weakness. But if you want to get free of your emotional jail, you have to dare yourself to open up to the pain of rejection. You aren't opening up for the benefit of the other; you are opening up for the freedom of your spirit's expression.

It is never appropriate to suppress or disregard how you are feeling. If you don't know how you feel, you cannot challenge those aspects, energies, and views that do not serve your development.

Where you feel guilt, remorse, anger, judgment, and sorrow, you will find an opportunity to grow.

Pain happens when you close, stuff down, identify with, act out, or shame the emotion. Emotions are neither good nor bad; they are a guiding tool to show you how you think about yourself and your life. Feeling strong emotions can be a signal for you to pay attention to the influences you are moving through and the thoughts you are thinking through in the moment.

Your thoughts are running a storyline of their own, twenty-four/seven, until you consciously stop and pay attention to whatever is taking over your awareness. Are your thoughts harsh and judgmental or kind and curious?

When your mind starts running in circles, gently remind yourself that you are more than your mind. You can quiet your mind chatter. Be kind to yourself. Welcome the chatter in, accept it with love, and then let it go. Practice this whenever you find your mind starting to spin, and soon your mind will begin to quiet. You will become much more present in the now and be able to make decisions with clarity.

Sometimes we are unsure of the forces within ourselves. Is it a feeling? Is it an emotion? Is it a way of being? Is it an influence? Our heads can spin with feeling overwhelmed in finding peace.

The force for me is this: As I have had no positive modeling of love, I create conflict with love and as love.

Self-inquiry: Ignoring love reinforces assuming the worst of me, but this makes me feel safe and mothered. Treating me well numbs me from assuming the best of me. Love's ideation brings me up and nurtures assuming the best of me, but I stifle the follow-through with acknowledging my husband's attention.

My husband and I were cuddling, talking about past relationships, when he said that I was "full of sexual tension" with my ex (my oldest son's father), and it was fully in the air when he was around. I would then get more sexually turned on and assertive with my sexual needs with my husband after being in my ex's presence.

As I contemplated this, it hit me that "tension" is what I associate love as—not the sexual act itself but the tension that comes with it. I had tension in all of my growing-up years, and when I got together with my husband, I was always trying to create tension. I would push him away from showing love. I would tell him he needed to get rough with me in the bedroom to get me turned on. I would try to pick a fight with him. With my ex, I associated the tension through the sex act as a demonstration of love.

Over the years, I associated a lack of tension between my husband and me as a boring, unloved, disinterested bonding that we struggled through.

When that awareness came to light, the doors to honest intimacy started to ground me with him in love.

Reject fear; choose love. This is a popular refrain. Many believe that there are only two primal emotions in human beings—love and fear—and that we cannot feel both at once, and that in the same way that light removes darkness, love can remove fear. *But could there be more?* Yes; I am informed that the opposite of love (at least for me) is inferiority and the two primal emotions in inferiority are "incomplete and pacify."

Incorporating a New Attribute

Wikipedia.com defines *attribute* as "a quality or feature regarded as a characteristic or inherent part of someone or something."

Four Attributes to the Viewing of Self in Life

1. Love—a diagnosis of equality to be consider real/complete/ important/significant. If you aren't in love, then you are indifferent.
2. Fear—control of assuming the best of your reality of value stifles importance and employs coping strategies that deviate from value. It's also referred to as "false evidence appearing real." If you are not in fear, then you have probably created an outcome of love.
3. Inadequacy—depression of self and not taking responsibility for restoring self-value, with a continual lack of equality to autonomy and allowing one to fit in and being valued. If you aren't inadequate, then you impact importance.
4. Indifference—unclear view of assuming the best of your reality of your value. If you aren't indifferent, you associate with self-satisfaction.

How you view yourself impacts the follow-through with assuming the best of your importance.

21

HOW TO CONQUER BOUNDARY-SETTING

PERSONAL BOUNDARIES ARE GUIDELINES, RULES, or limits that people create to identify reasonable, safe, and permissible ways for other people to behave toward them and in response to someone failing to regard those limits.

All healthy relationships have boundaries, as they have defined where one person ends and the other begins. Each person is clear as to "what is mine and what is yours." They have defined what is right for them and what will feel wrong if it is encountered, as they have given thought to their personal safety, value, and rights ahead of time.

Boundaries are about letting go of the worry toward what the response from others will be, such as always wondering, "Will they like me or won't they?"

When you can allow information, experiences, and attitudes in, without taking it personally and without trying to control a specific outcome from happening, then you can easily discern for yourself if you want to let the information in or not. You know whether it will serve you or not. Ask yourself: "Will this be a benefit or a liability for me if I choose to accept it (or not)?"

If you are not dependent on validation from others or something else, you can allow yourself to let go of needing life to show up in a certain way. You would not expect people to treat you one way so you will like them or to know that they liked you.

You are confident in yourself and know what benefits you and what will become a liability if you proceed further with it. You make smart choices for yourself, and you expect the same from others. Boundaries become about what is best for you and others.

A lot of us, though, grew up walking on eggshells and feeling insecure with how to relate to the environment around us. We didn't know when we were treading on sensitive ground as there was no clear structure. We didn't always know what was acceptable and what wasn't. Sometimes, our behavior was tolerated; other times it was resented. We had our guards up. We didn't trust easily, as we expected to receive disapproval in any given moment.

Survival mode became our primitive way of being.

Signs of Unhealthy Boundaries

- Telling all
- Trusting no one; trusting everyone; black-and-white thinking
- Not noticing when someone displays weak boundaries
- Not noticing when someone invades your boundaries
- Sharing too much personal stuff at the first meeting
- Being overwhelmed by a person but staying close by
- Acting on the first sexual impulse
- Being sexual for your partner, not yourself
- Going against personal values or rights to please another person
- Falling in love with someone who reaches out
- Falling in love with a new acquaintance
- Accepting food, gifts, touch, or sex that you don't want
- Touching a person without asking
- Taking as much as you can for the sake of getting
- Letting others define you
- Letting others direct your life
- Letting others describe your reality
- Believing others can anticipate your needs
- Expecting others to fill your needs automatically
- Allowing someone to take as much as he or she can from you
- Falling apart so someone will take care of you
- Experiencing sexual and physical abuse
- Experiencing food abuse

Signs of Healthy Boundaries

- Appropriate trust
- Moving step by step into intimacy
- Staying focused on your own growth and recovery
- Maintaining personal values, no matter what others want
- Revealing a little bit of yourself at a time and checking to see how the other person responds to your sharing
- Putting a new acquaintance on hold until you check for compatibility
- Deciding whether a potential relationship will be good for you
- Weighing the consequences before acting on sexual impulse
- Noticing when someone else has inappropriate boundaries
- Being sexual when you want to be sexual; concentrating hard on your own pleasure, rather than monitoring reactions of your partner
- Asking people for permission before you touch them
- Trusting your own decisions
- Defining your truth as you see it
- Knowing who you are and what you want
- Becoming your own loving parent
- Talking to yourself with gentleness, humor, love, and respect
- Respecting others; not taking advantage of someone's generosity
- Having self-respect; not giving too much, hoping someone will like you
- Not allowing someone to take advantage of your generosity
- Recognizing that friends and partners are not mind readers
- Clearly communicating your wants and needs while recognizing that you can get turned down (You can ask, though.)

Weak Boundaries

- Saying yes, without thinking if that works
- Avoiding speaking up at all costs, as you believe that will create conflict

- Accepting everything (whatever you want, I want; whatever you do, I do; whatever you think is right, I will agree that it's right)
- Giving in; *no* is not an option

Strong Boundaries

Saying *no* without listening or considering
    Making it all about "safety and protection"
    Thinking you will hurt me if the wall comes down, so the wall stays up
    Staying at arm's length; lack of intimacy, trust, support
    Pushing away before I can get hurt

Healthy Boundaries

Following clearly defined and respected boundaries
    Forming them from a place of self-knowledge (You know who you are, what you will accept for yourself, what you value, how you want to be treated, and how you want to treat others.)

If you currently have weak boundaries, creating healthy boundaries can be scary. It takes time to establish them. Notice, without judgment, when you have neglected a boundary, and then, in your head, replay that scenario and define that boundary. You will be ready the next time to implement another stronger step toward boundary-setting.

With patience and understanding, a space for respectful discussion can open up. This can happen only if the person on the other end is open and willing to make that shift for himself or herself because that person will need to adjust to your new and defined sense of self.

If a person doesn't show you positive regard, respect, or acknowledgement of your new and defined boundaries, then maybe you need to define a strict boundary of separation for yourself. It is okay to let go of a relationship, especially if it involves mean, discouraging, spiteful, suspicious, envious, manipulative, and disapproving attitudes toward you. Just because someone is your mother, father, lover, sibling, or friend does not mean you must allow them to take their disrespectful attitude out on you. You deserve more. It is right for you to take back your space, your mind, your emotions, and your love for self. No one has the right to disrespect you, no matter their relationship to you.

Do not appease them; be the first to pacify, apologize, give a compliment, and/or make peace. Allow them time to respond and to ask for forgiveness or clarity. How serious are they in admitting their attitudes? You lose power when you appease, as you are trying to prove that you are good enough to be valued by them. (Damn it! You are good enough—and always have been. Let's reclaim that!)

Consider that it does take time for adjustment, though. The other person may push back against your new boundaries to test how serious you are. Be clear about why you are making the boundaries and be prepared to stand your ground. I don't mean you should get physical or start an argument, but don't go back to your weak boundaries. It should get easier. If it doesn't, then you may need to make the choice to separate.

I found out for myself that separation worked, so I could free up space to work on myself.

Note: It is hard to discern disrespect in families, as it is ingrained in the fabric of your relationships. As children, we learn to get into a role of caretaking the parent's emotional needs so the parent's way of being toward us (discouragement, disrespect, disapproval) becomes the "mothering" that we, as a child, become dependent on to affirm our self-identification.

Then we move into an intimate relationship and repeat the same behaviors of giving in, doing more for our partners than for ourselves, being emotionally disconnected, not speaking up, and not standing our ground, as we have no set boundaries within.

We don't want to hurt the other person's feelings, as we have learned that his or her feelings are more important than our own feelings. We possibly learned that speaking up creates conflict, and we don't want to bear that responsibility, so we learn to appease. But appeasing by taking responsibility for the impact of others shuts us down to our own interpretation of what is personally encountered. Guilt takes over, as we believe that we are responsible for the outcome.

It takes separating from the other person to get clear, get real with ourselves, build our backbone strong, and get down to the business of creating boundaries that serve us.

Ask Yourself

- What are my values? What will I stand up for?
- How do I want to respond when _____ happens?
- How do I want others to respond to me? What will I not take from them?
- Am I emotionally disconnected? Do I escape or become numb when loved ones get needy?

Define what support will entail, and claim it for yourself.

22

HOW DO YOU MAINTAIN YOUR WAY OF LIFE?

SELF-PRESERVATION: INSTINCTS BY MEANS OF which people maintain their own existence

- Believing something is futile
- Perceiving that you are unable to move forward
- High-functioning depression
- Holding a belief of "I'm not enough"

Self-preservation stops progress. It keeps you limited, untrusting, shut down, unfocused, and lacking purpose. These habits keep you from loving and believing in yourself, and this mind-set stops you in your tracks.

Maintaining

Subconsciously, you can develop one or more underlying fears:

- Fear of rejection
- Fear of criticism
- Fear of abandonment
- Fear of aloneness
- Fear of failure/success
- Fear of exposure/embarrassment
- Fear of being wrong
- Fear of being seen or heard

Through this fear, you would form patterns of social-coping behaviors:

- Unsocial/withdrawn
- Resentful
- Suspicious
- Fearful/anxious
- Easily discouraged/procrastinating
- Overly critical of others
- Sensitive
- Suggestible
- Controlling/dominating
- Lazy
- Judgmental

You form defense mechanisms:

- Denial
- Rationalization
- Blame
- Repression
- Compliance
- Intellectualization
- Manipulation
- Punishment
- Domination

Emotional Coping mechanisms range from being clingy to keeping a safe distance (emotional withdrawal, collapse, or detachment).

You start making rules:

If you loved me you wouldn't …

If you loved me, you would …

Prove that you love me (because I don't believe I am loveable).

> "If you are not eternally showing me that you live
> for me, then I feel like I am nothing."
> —Virginia Stair

The outcome is control—you try hard to control self (emotions), others, and environment (God).

The impact is that you form a dependency on others and circumstances to provide prestige, security, and love.

You try to have a sense of security and safety by regulating how you think others should treat you, but as long as you are emotionally dependent on someone, you will never view the world as a safe and supportive place. Waiting nervously for that one time when the person won't live up to your expectations will leave you feeling alone and defeated.

Breathe. Don't beat yourself up; instead, take this journey as an adventure into discovering what the past held so that you can find the healing and wisdom in it.

Relax and Reflect

> Create a timeline on a piece of paper—birth to nine years, ages ten to fourteen, fifteen to nineteen, young adult, adult. Write out your life's significant experiences and *your* accompanying emotions, associations, or assumptions (the view) that you attached to each experience.
> What are the connections? What are the themes? What are the impacts?
> What are the lasting effects?
> How do you act out as a consequence? What do you try to control moving forward?
> What do you hold to be true, coming from this experience?
> What decisions did you make with regard to yourself and what you expect for yourself? How do you expect the world to treat you?
> Do you struggle with receiving positive attention from others?
> Do you fear being judged, and it holds you back from revealing much about you?
> What pattern of disturbance keeps arising in your life? Peel the layers; what is the underlying limiting belief? Note that it isn't the disturbance that affects you, as it is the filter through which you

are viewing the disturbance. If you change your inner filter, your view of the disturbance will change.

➢ Through this belief, what fear keeps holding you back from living with an open, full heart?

➢ What defense mechanisms do you use to hide your fears?

➢ What control patterns are expressed through this disturbance?

➢ How do you perform to gain people's attention?

➢ How do you compare yourself to others? Do you compare your children with others?

➢ What rules dominate your household? Were they made out of trust and love or doubt and fear?

➢ Admit your emotional dependency. What or who do you need to fill your love tank, and how is that shown? Does the dependency not allow someone else to fully live his or her life?

➢ Do you have a hard time saying no to someone's request? Why? Keep asking why with each answer given until you get to the core of your resistance to loving yourself.

Moving Forward

Say, "I choose to intentionally wipe clean my emotional backdrop of all systemic, familial, and generational traumas of inferiority and distortions."

With what do you need to come to terms? Accept it.

Say, "I give myself permission to engage in following through on supporting an alignment with self-importance, as it is my right to be equal in value, existing."

Say, "My truth represents empowered subjectivity to bring me up through the existence of my reality as genuine."

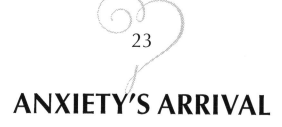

23

ANXIETY'S ARRIVAL

ANXIETY IS A FEELING OF worry, nervousness, or unease, typically about an imminent event or something with an uncertain outcome. There is a desire to do something, typically accompanied by unease. It can be triggered by encountering a personal sense of being, feeling, or doing "wrongness," which looks like the following:

- Feeling abandoned
- Fear of outshining others
- Perceived judgment from others
- Shame (feeling like you bring the bigger burden to people's lives)

When the trigger arises, you channel that energy into anxiety out of self-preservation, as it is too much to handle. The underlying belief is that, "It's inadequate to be complete within myself."

It's an inner pull between being annoying to others and being assertive in your sense of self.

Anxiety is triggered when you step away from objectivity to own your power of subjectivity.

The Meaning of Anxiety

It is a duty to the system to not liberate from a trapped_____ (mind-set, nurturance, earning your keep, if only, I am more than). This part of you wants to be free and nurturing on the whole but is held back by duty to appease the system (system of family, friends, church, work, school, and politics).

To release yourself from the symptoms of anxiety, breathe slowly and methodically. Focus on what you can perceive with your senses. What can you touch? What can you see? What can you smell? What can you hear?

When you are at home and comfortable, in a few moments of silence, reflect on what you were thinking of, working on, or experiencing when anxiety rose within you. Uncover what is objective, and make the switch to subjectivity.

Anxiety and Panic

Anxiety is what always came up for me, but that's because I didn't have the word *panic* in my consciousness yet. It was a post on a friend's timeline that urged me to look it up.

What I realized was that the blackout I'd experienced at a workshop was a panic attack, arising from the anxiety I'd been feeling all morning. When I landed in the emergency room, the doctor didn't diagnose me. I had to use Wise Core Consulting to help me uncover the answers I was unconsciously looking for and then trust in the validity of what came up.

What Are Panic Attacks?

Wikipedia.com states that panic attacks are sudden, intense surges of fear, panic, or anxiety. They are overwhelming, and they have physical as well as emotional symptoms. Many people who experience panic attacks may have difficulty breathing, sweat profusely, tremble, and feel their hearts pounding. Some people also experience chest pain and a feeling of detachment from reality or from themselves during a panic attack, so they make think they're having a heart attack. Others have reported feeling as if they are having a stroke.

For me, it was blacking out, but before I did, I could feel energy rising in my chest area.

Resources and support will give you symptoms and exercises to deal with the symptoms, but they don't know what the underlying meaning is; this is what I hope to share with you in the following pages.

Panic is default.
Default is "failure in a duty." I fail in my duty to me.

24

CUT THE CHAINS THAT HOLD YOU HOSTAGE

WHAT IS FORGIVENESS? GENERALLY, FORGIVENESS is a decision to let go of resentment, judgment, and thoughts of revenge and accountability. The act that hurt or offended you might always remain a part of your energetic imprinting, but forgiveness can lessen its grip on you and can help you focus on other positive parts of your life.

Note: If you were emotionally abused, the most damaging mistake you can make is to invest your time, effort, and resources in the "rehabilitation" of the abuser. Trying to fix that person will likely not change him or her, which will leave you taking on the blame, believing that you deserve no better. The abuser has no right to forgiveness; it has to be earned, as actions speak louder than words.

Forgiveness doesn't mean that you deny the other person's responsibility for hurting you, and it doesn't minimize or justify the wrong. You can forgive the person without excusing the act. Forgiveness brings a kind of peace that helps you go on with life. Letting go of grudges and bitterness can make way for compassion, kindness, and peace.

Forgiveness will not be possible until you have compassion in your heart, and it starts by demonstrating it to yourself first. By hanging on to this feeling of having been unjustly treated, you end up hurting yourself by keeping your anger brewing inside. The worst part is that the person who hurt you has gone on with his or her life, having no thought of the pain that you find yourself drowning in. You are hurting yourself and giving your power away to the one you perceive has hurt you.

Another part of forgiveness is in realizing that you were a part of the problem too, as it takes two to create a relationship. How did you handle yourself? Take responsibility, and atone for it.

Step out of the facade. Become the observer of your feelings and thoughts. Don't judge or criticize your thoughts; this keeps you stuck, and it keeps the mind in protection mode. Just be in a state of curiosity. Pour a cup of tea and open up a dialogue with your mind. Tell it that you appreciate how it has taken care of you and that it is okay to take a break, as you are safe and well cared for.

When you criticize and judge yourself, your lower self acts out even stronger, as it thinks you're being attacked—remember that its job is to protect you. But you don't need the protection of a scared lower self; you need self-forgiveness, with compassion from your higher self or heart space.

You are of heart spirit, and it connects you with all of life. It is safe to surrender to that power within. When you step out of the lower self, become the observer, and start to question the collective beliefs and values, you slowly release the bindings of distrust and insecurities. You start to allow transparency of the authentic you to shine out.

Love is exposed in trust. As you start to trust in your spirit, your intuition, that instinctive knowledge or insight starts to blossom. And that's when life really becomes an adventure of discovery and destiny.

Judging another and judging yourself are the same error. Demonstrate gentleness and loving kindness toward yourself. Ease back on the self-judgment; as you do, you'll find you judge others less.

Do you remember a time when you felt a presence within you? Was there ever a time when you knew that no matter what, you couldn't do any wrong? Sit back and breathe those feelings to the surface. Feel them and integrate with them.

25

HOW TO CLEAR
LIMITING BELIEFS

ACKNOWLEDGE LIMITING SELF-BELIEFS. RECOGNIZE THAT they are objective, as they came from others projecting their stress onto you. You did not know how to digest the information so you internalized it and took it on as a personal trait.

Examples

➤ "I am a mistake at connecting to my significance." Turn it around as, "It was a mistake that they didn't encourage me to connect to my significance to self-imagine."

➤ "I am stupid and can't get anything right!" Turn it around as, "It was discouraging for me to not get the support I needed to believe in my capabilities."

➤ "Nobody loves me." Turn it around as, "I was neglected, and my sense of worth was not nurtured to thrive. So today, I struggle with intimacy, as I didn't learn to perceive care from others."

➤ "I have no power." Turn it around as, "My tendency to depress encouraging self-efficacy is an effect of discouragement to be adequate in being critical in recognizing the projections of others."

Once you shift from objective ownership to subjective ownership of your life, you can instill the belief that you are smart and capable of connecting to defining what being "good enough within" means to you.

When you feel any challenge with releasing from stuck emotions, mind-sets, and beliefs, do the following:

> Feel your bodily discomfort (this feels different for each of us—tight neck muscles, sore lower back, clenched jaw, burning sensation in your belly). Where do you hold your stress? Put an emotion to the bodily feeling.

> Ask it, "What do you want me to know?" Be patient in waiting for the answer.

> Know what your triggers are. What happens that brings you instantly back to the feeling of insecurity, resistance, self-judgment, or guilt?

> Ask yourself, "What am I unwilling to let go of? What do I fear will happen? What am I afraid of losing?"

> Breathe in peace; breathe out pain. Say the mantra, "Peace in; pain out."

> Focus on your breath; it is life, and where there is life, there is hope. Focusing on your breath brings you into the present; it releases you from the mind and connects you with your heart space of spirit. Spirit is heart. Spirit is love. Spirit is truth.

> Change false beliefs into new truths. If you do not feel love, light, abundance, and trust, then you are in resistance.

The following scenario is an example of the process you can use with a resistance or block you are experiencing:

Someone tells you that you're not doing something right. You feel frustration rising in your chest. Your thought says that you are stupid and can't do anything right. You want to react by attacking with an insult, but instead, you look at this situation as a chance to demonstrate acceptance for yourself and the situation.

Step 1: You allow the emotion to rise by feeling it. "I feel tightness in my chest." Don't judge it, own it, or identify with it; just observe it as an outsider and feel it.

Step 2: Acknowledge the limiting, false belief, which is the subconscious program, "This is the mind, but I am not the mind."

Step 3: Replace it with a truthful affirmation of your choice: "I am capable. I am worthy. And I am not alone in this."

Step 4: Say with intensity, "Thank you, [*insert your name*]. I forgive you for thinking less of yourself, and I love you." You will feel your energy mellow out. You will feel compassion. This is the space in which healing starts to happen.

Once you find yourself in a space of peace, your next move is to inquire if there was any truth to the comment. Remind yourself that this is a process. Go easy on yourself. Many of your messages were developed in childhood, and the body is still hanging on to them.

This is a process of lovingly allowing your inner child to share with you messages that do not serve you any longer. Your past wants to release the old to allow a fresh view to develop. Allow any shame and guilt with which you have associated yourself to release and leave.

Now you can inquire: "Was this comment made to show me where I can make improvements, or was it an attack against me?" Now you have some real information to work with. Now you can respond with compassion and respect for yourself and understanding for how you feel and care so you can speak up with self-confidence.

If you think that others attacked you, you can ask yourself, "Why would they attack me?" What would be their benefit in attacking you? Is there any truth to that? What insecurity is it poking at? If you think it's about making improvements, you can say, "I'm unsure what you meant by your comment, so I want to double-check to clarify what you were trying to express to me." By taking responsibility for your interpretation, you will have embraced your power and will open the doors to creating a purposeful solution. You can then offer a positive reply: "I would love to problem-solve a way to make this situation work for both of us."

With consistency, you will change the conditioning that formed limiting mind-sets, and in its place, you will input a new program in your brain that will serve you to its fullest.

26

DEMAND MORE FOR YOURSELF

IF YOU LEARNED TO HIDE or camouflage your abilities as a child, by the time you got to adulthood, you would have denied expression of your most unique and passionate parts of yourself. You've learned that these aspects of yourself threaten your safety, and you need to play small (depress the real self from shining out), but they are the direct path to love and living out your destiny.

You can get so used to life showing up in a certain way that to move beyond that can seem too risky. You don't know what to expect, so you stay safe and play small. You expect and settle for just so much for yourself.

On a piece of paper, write out your issue or pain. Then draw out five columns and label them with the points listed below. Write your responses in the columns to uncover whatever situation holds you back from truly expressing yourself:

- List the negative costs of having your issue or pain.
- What is your payoff (reinforcement) for hanging on to the pain or issue?
- What are your fears of moving forward?
- What can you look forward to by stepping away from your issue?
- What are you willing to let in? Give yourself permission to receive everything good.

When you don't love yourself and appreciate that you have strengths, gifts, and abilities to share with others, you're left with a sense of emptiness, sadness, loneliness, and uncertainty. This learned shame and fear around your most vulnerable and valuable attributes is often a huge effect of pop culture, marketing initiatives, and childhood conditioning and influences. The best— sometimes, the only—way out of this shame and doubt about you is through relationships that support and nourish the most vulnerable part of self.

Of the people you know, who knows the real you?
Who isn't too envious of your gifts, talents, strengths, or personality?
Who can encourage you to express the natural you?

If you aren't sure what your gifts or talents are, try to do something out of the ordinary. Did you pick it up easily? Did you enjoy it? If so, what qualities did you like about it, and why did you like them? Keep experimenting until you try something that fits you well.

You tend to choose the people in your life based on how you think and feel about yourself. A simple example: if you smoke and drink, you will find company to hang out with to pursue those activities. If you decide to quit smoking or drinking, you will naturally find new company to hang around with and will pursue new activities to fill the void.

The same goes for making new friends or dating. Depending where you are on the self-awareness and trust scale, you will pick a friend or partner who reflects those qualities you unconsciously think you need and deserve in the relationship. The more you grow as a person, the more the qualities of your friends or partner will change. The giving and receiving will naturally balance out as the relationship's needs and wants balance out. Recognize what progress has been made to let these people in, and celebrate letting go of people who do not serve your development.

With the encouragement of those who care and respect you, you will have the freedom to allow your true self to express itself. Over time, as you allow your learned shame and fear to fade away, your trust in your gifts will naturally rise to the surface and take shape. As you release the false beliefs about your worth and your capabilities, your level of deserving will naturally increase, and manifesting your heart's desires will start to unfold.

The world needs examples of people who have come alive! So ask yourself what makes you come alive. What values did your family hold most important, and how did they express them?

- Are you living out those same values? Do they resonate with you, or do you need to replace them?
- Do you believe that you need "permission" to move forward with your life? If you do, give it to yourself because your permission is the only one you need.
- How would you feel if you had more success than your parents, made more money, were happier in your relationships, and had no limits on yourself?
- Where are you holding yourself back from receiving?
- Have you sat down to clarify what your needs are and how you want to get them met? Do you feel that you deserve to receive positive outcomes?
- What would it take to raise the limit that you have set for yourself?
- What parts of yourself are you holding back from showing others out of fear of disapproval?
- What part of your life demonstrates a low set point of value? How can you raise your set point to create more value?

27

CEASE CONTROL; LET LIFE FLOW

WHAT DOES IT MEAN TO let life flow? A free-flowing mode of being means that you are not caught up in the should-have/could-have/would-have mentality. You don't feel guilty for not having done a specific activity, and you don't try to control an outcome (you don't need things to turn out a certain way). You learn to let go of your idea of what any given moment is going to be as you allow the moment to unravel before you. Do you feel safe in allowing follow-through?

You learn to be flexible, instead of rigid or demanding. You learn to receive change and uncertainty with curiosity, instead of fearing it. As things arise, you adapt and let go of set plans and goals. You are free to do this because you trust where you might end up. You just want to be present in your journey, be compassionate with each step, and possibly learn something about yourself along the way. The destination becomes irrelevant. If you feel acceptance within the moment, then how can there be judgment or expectation? Each step along the way becomes the destination, and it is exactly where you should be. Breathe into the moment and appreciate what is being offered. Do you trust that others assume the best of you?

How do you know if you've made the right decision when you need to make a choice? How do you feel inside? Do you feel restrictive in your breathing, with tight neck muscles or a clenched jaw; essentially feeling heavy, unsure, or fearful? Or do you feel light, hopeful, and excited to start, with full-belly breathing and a sense of optimism or curiosity, wondering "What if?" Do you assume and trust the best of yourself?

When you are struggling with something, ask yourself, "Is this an influence? Do I feel safe?" Safety strengthens certainty, which influences relaxed living.

If you aren't sure what to do when making a decision, put your hand over your heart, breathe deeply through the belly, and ask, "Am I making decisions out of love and trust or fear and doubt?" Be careful, as an influence can trick you into believing you are doing something out of love. Challenge each response you make. Ask "Is it true?"; keep asking until you get to the core reason. Do you expect the best for yourself?

28

COMMUNICATION IS KEY

TO SUCCESSFULLY COMMUNICATE WITH OTHERS, you must first learn to communicate with yourself.

Intrapersonal communication is the most basic level of communication; it is an activity that occurs within your own body. Your emotions are the first indicator that you are thinking thoughts that are unkind, judgmental, or based in lack, meaning that you don't have enough of whatever you think you need to be happy. When you understand the identity you have taken on, your belief system changes, your thought process improves, and you are able to make better life choices for yourself.

As you may have learned to ignore what is happening within your internal environment, journaling can be a perfect companion for intra-reflection, as it gets you to slow down and settle into whatever is trying to rise from within.

Developing effective intrapersonal communication takes discipline and a willingness to slow down your day enough to hear your own thoughts.

By first understanding how communication relies on your own particular perceptions and assumptions, you then will be able to fully understand the way that society communicates in your daily life. Your intrapersonal communication reveals itself in how you think things through, interpret events, interpret messages of others, respond to your own experiences, and respond to your interactions with others.

People seldom share precisely the same perceptions because no two people have the same filters of how to relate and respond. Two people in the same room can have completely different perceptions of the same event. Each sibling, as well as the parents of a family, has his or her own take on the experience of growing up together. These varying perceptions can cause conflict and misunderstanding. To overcome this, you must continually check your own perceptions, and make sure they are accurate and valid by checking them against the other person's perceptions.

Be open-minded to challenging your perceptions.

Never assume that what you perceive as the truth is the actual, absolute truth.

Communication is both comprehension (the understanding of the inflow) and expression (the outflow) of information, opinions, ideas, and desires. Be clear!

For an *intrapersonal* perception, check and question what you sense in your body—what information could have been dismissed, as well as your personal understanding of what you perceive to be true.

For an *interpersonal* perception, check and ask the other person if what you heard was what he or she was trying to convey. Then analyze that person's point of view to see if there is a place for you to take responsibility for how you perceive things.

When you want to share significant information about yourself, consider the purpose of the self-disclosure and your communication goals.

- What do you hope to gain?
- What is your intention? *Are you trying to prove something?*

Building of Intimacy

Healthy communication is a way of expressing needs, wants, and feelings in a safe and respectful manner. It takes vulnerability to self-disclose something that is sensitive, and if you are met with derision or disinterest, something tender shrivels and retracts within you, making you think twice about sharing that part again.

Deep intimacy can only be bared and shared when both parties risk letting go to reveal the inner most truth of self.

Only when the curtain of judgment, rules, and demands is stripped away will you find the capacity to open up to really know yourself and the other person. For instance, when you don't take your partner's behavior as an attack on your self-worth, you are able to allow him or her the chance to clearly understand himself or herself and express thoughts and emotions in a healthy way.

Doing this allows you to step back from orchestrating a certain outcome for yourself. You are able to focus on what is offered to you, rather than on what you wish would be offered back.

Identifying the real reasons behind complaints and arguments takes a willingness to hear, through compassion and understanding. When you open up to being vulnerable in communicating your needs, you open up to embracing love and intimacy.

With curiosity, ask yourself:

- What did my parents' relationship look like or model to me?
- How do I demonstrate care and love to those who are closest to me?
- What keeps me from truly being present to those who are important to me?
- What am I afraid my partner might find out about me? What am I hiding from? What am I afraid will happen?
- What do I want from my partner that will help me feel safe, wanted, and respected?

Be truthful with yourself, and you will be set free.

The Language of Sexuality

Throughout this book, you have been paying attention to what you've been taught to think and feel about yourself in life. Your sexuality is a huge component of how you see yourself in the big picture of life, as well as with all other areas of your life. Your view of sexuality has been influenced by your parents, teachers, friends, and the media. It is a fundamental aspect of an individual's personality or identity.

Sexuality involves the whole person: body, mind, and spirit and higher self. The need for love and for close and trusting relationships is fundamental to being human. The key to intimacy is the closeness, acceptance, and trust that exists between two people, not whether they are sexually involved.

Early in life, it's important to form close relationships with family members and friends who are emotionally and spiritually intimate but that involve no sexual activity. These relationships will lead to healthy adult sexuality of love and intimacy.

Sexuality, as a language of love, draws people out of themselves and toward each other.

If you are assured that you are loved, then there is little risk and little to lose. Relationships would seem less scary and judgmental, going into them. You never may have had that chance to form trust in yourself because of the abusive actions and destructive influences of others, but know that it is never too late to do so. It will take surrendering in the moment to gain a clear understanding of what you are feeling, thinking, and perceiving and then asking yourself if this way serves you or not. Be patient, as it takes time to build up trust.

Personal Reflection

The only image I have of love between my dad and mom is at the kitchen counter, when he walked up from behind her to wrap his arms around her. She looked back at him with a disappointing scowl and a slew of disapproval coming through her words.

My four-year-old self interpreted that scenario as, "He is a failure at showing love."

My higher self interpreted it as seeing my dad abandoned of beloved (his wife shutting him down) showed that his love didn't make a difference to the value he had to give.

And this is the interpretation that follows me into adulthood and influences every intimate relationship into which I put effort.

I have realized that I need to feel safe in my relationships, and that's why I chose to marry my husband. He was the first partner with whom I felt safe. But he has pointed out his confusion with me and my past; he wonders how safety can be my number-one need, yet I never played safe. The main lack of safety for me was having unprotected sex.

I've lived my life without considering personal safety. I was processed as being a nobody. I was confused as to what I should expect as an expression of love to self and from others. If I am a nobody, why would I give consideration to my own personal enjoyment or safety?

29

GRIEF

AT THE CORE OF THE belief that "I am a mistake, and I bring a bigger burden" is the emotional suffering known as grief.

When you have been discouraged from holding value for yourself, a deep sorrow at this loss of self-significance buries itself within you. When you do the work of restoring your significance, a deep sadness will arise, partly because of what you lost in your childhood and partly because of your care toward yourself.

The care you demonstrate toward yourself is foreign; it doesn't seem natural, as the natural way of being has been to disconnect to the experience of nurturing. Be with the sadness and know it is a natural response of care.

There is a void within if you did not receive the nurturing of care, love, and encouragement that you needed. When the love, acceptance, care, and validation show, tears can rise up, as it signifies a release of the pain of what was denied to you but also a thankfulness that it has arrived.

Despair is the emotion that keeps hanging on. Despair is the complete loss or absence of hope. Following despair, you can expect to feel anger, but the emotion is actually bitterness, which is anger and disappointment at being treated unfairly; it acts like resentment.

What have you lost? What was denied to you? What do you regret? What can't you let go of?

Forgive yourself for taking ownership of the pain. Now give yourself permission to let it go.

Regret

Today, I see myself as separate components of value—do you too?—because I learned to compartmentalize being real vs. being less real. I learned that being real and whole meant being "broken"; that was an effect of my wounded childhood scripting. Believing the viewpoints of others became real, but it became a false sense of relating to my truth. The truth is that I am whole, and all the points of subjectivity, not objectivity, form my identity.

Regret has me compartmentalizing (separating from parts of myself) because when I detached emotionally, I started to deny consciousness (being awake and aware) of my significance.

I learned that my power *to be* is futile, as I believe I have sabotaged proving myself worthy. I struggle with paying attention to self-significance, as I believe I am unworthy to connect to my consciousness of completeness, so I regress into disapproving of myself.

Moving forward, regret lingers with self-blame that spurs exasperated inaction. The perception that hangs in the stale air is, "Why me? I have done wrong, and I can't change this." Holding on to being the victim of circumstances takes over the right to let go and move on. I have mental and emotional discomfort and anxiety, as I collided with not being good enough for someone or something I deemed important. I must heal the need to prove myself worthy. I am worthy.

You are worthy and always have been. Change your inner dialogue to one of acceptance. Move forward with a willingness to anticipate acting awake and aware of what you feel, what you contribute, and what you can control.

It is time to reclaim our power, value, and significance so that we can subjectively live in the now. We must integrate all the disconnected parts of who we are so we can be whole and feel complete.

Self-Care Activities

Trauma quickens your physiological response. Trauma causes you to perceive certain life experiences (triggers) as a threat. Your body reacts with fight, flight, or freeze.

Learn what triggers you. Realize that it is only a memory of an experience; it is not literally happening to you in the present moment.

Tune in to your environment. Once you know what triggers you, you can pay attention to what brings you back to calm.

What Cues You to Calm?

In the conflict stage, you want to protect yourself and survive.

In the calm state, you naturally will want to eat well, play, rest, sleep, move, exercise, journal, visit with people, get outside, and learn to be with yourself. I would suggest adding yoga and meditation.

Yoga is a yielding to acknowledging adequacy in "being" within the moment and "doing" within the movements.

Meditation encourages love for self and connection with the Creator. I meditate by taking walks in nature. Words of inspiration come so easily to me in these spots of oneness. Connection happens in a state of conscious awareness. I can be aware yet not quite conscious (awake) to the truth (which is where I am). But I am always willing to be open to receiving that which will support me into conscious reality.

The act of love resides in the head space of creating and accomplishing and the heart space of feeling and knowing. Everything else (patience, joy, acceptance, purpose, peace) has dual presence in the head and heart. One can be closed off from the experience of the other. Balance is in the connection to both.

Know that a spiritual practice is more than just sitting, stretching, and meditating. The practice of living is in the focus we put toward looking, touching, thinking, eating, moving, and talking. The intention of every breath, act, decision, and attachment can help us become more of who we are.

30

JUDGMENT

Right Judgment

RIGHT JUDGMENT IS NEEDED, AS it's about being good enough to be seen and heard in self-advocating the right to be, which represents nurturing a mind-set of being value.

You know your value, being more real and being significant, and you stand up for what is right for you through boundary-setting.

Defensive Judgment

You become overly anxious to protect yourself against criticism (threats). This judgment has you act in response to not being good enough, instead of knowing your value and standing up for what is right and dismissing what feels wrong. Being good enough becomes a hard lesson in appeasing the systemic (the way it is done) superiority, instead of an easier lesson in being good enough.

What Defensive Judgment Looks Like

- Anger
- Bitterness
- Self-pity
- Suspicions
- Replicating past drama
- Isolation
- Threatening our existence
- Justification
- Lying

- Avoidance
- Persecution
- Injustice
- Resistance
- Victimhood
- Proving yourself
- Moodiness
- Criticism
- Hostility

I impact my ability to bring myself up and live true to myself by reliving these effects of judgment.

Effects of Defensive Judgment:

- Inferiority
- Less real
- Undervalued
- Being the injustice of not being good enough

The beliefs that

o I am a mistake (incomplete).
o I am a bigger burden.
o Something is wrong with me.
o I am not special (lack purpose).
o I am inadequate.
o I am useless.
o I am only good for one thing.
o I am not enough.
o I am too stupid.
o I am unlovable.
o I shouldn't have been born.

31

THE MEANING OF FAMILY AND HOME

FAMILY IS MEANT TO EMPOWER the "superiority of self" by assuming the best of the "soul tie" of autonomy being equal. *Soul tie* is the connection of each other being equal, as part of the whole.

Home is about empowering autonomy to attach to elevating self-importance as subjectivity, plus a soul tie of nourishing superiority through the support of each other's reality being of value. Home is where you learn how to love, care, support, and encourage each other to grow up and move forward into your best sense of self and where you can expect to get all that in return, as being an equal unit of the whole.

This is very important for parents to understand!

The mother and the father should both be on the same page of modeling the importance of assuming the best of the child's being equal to their partnership. On the foundation of equality, it offers support of a primal mode of contributing to the progress of the duality of feminine and masculine being equal in the alignment with assuming the best of one's value. Being complete comes through in the interconnectedness of the feminine and masculine energy being equal in value.

The Mother/Father Duality

We, as a society, burden the mother presence as being unequal in the raising of her children. As we persecute her style of support, we lose focus of her nurture's (breastfeeding) integrity. We cannot cure ourselves of the shaming we do to duality, as it is the primal mode of systemic inferiority we live by.

Primal mode represents something primitive, primary, or fundamental.

Which came first—the chicken or the egg? In the same context of arrival, which came first—society's shaming of being inferior or being "equality in duality" in supporting completeness?

No one should intrude on the partnership of raising a child in the equality of duality.

As a society, we need to change how we judge the parenting of others— from the name that is chosen, to the colors a child wears, to breastfeeding in public, to the choice of toys to play with, to the father staying home on paternity leave, to whom they choose to love. There is no judgment that hurts like a society that has a black-and-white view of what is acceptable and what is not.

Childhood injury follows into adulthood and causes havoc in a more mature way.

Up until now, I have shared with you what I have learned for myself; but I have just skimmed the surface of what ails me/us in our existence. *How do I know this?* Because I don't feel clear, light, or resurrected in myself.

Yes, the past is gone, but imprints of the womb unknowingly influence us.

Follow me as I delve deeper into self, as I use the reflections I have shared to get clear on what is blocking the self from living free. Revelations I am sure will be exposed. It is just a matter of time.

Part Two

Realizing the Duality of Our Existence

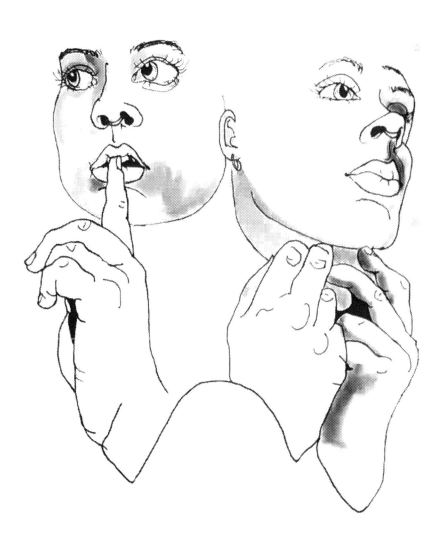

PREFACE

I HAVE ALWAYS WORKED WITH people in a variety of different capacities. I have owned three businesses, but most often, I listen to people's problems. I sat for hours, listening to my grandma and doing some of the same with my mom, and it flowed into my relationships with others.

What I have heard is that people feel incomplete. But what do they perceive is missing within themselves or throughout their lives?

I learned of this missing paradigm of wellness when I became so overwhelmed with life that I didn't care if I lived. I was incorporating radical self-care yet struggled with maintaining my sanity and a sense of equality in relationships. I felt toxic in my relationships, as I was confused as to what should feel right for me.

I'm not sure when I started to write everything down, but at one point, I decided that I was writing a book on how to release the past to become your best self. The more I got into my material and the more I talked with people, the more I realized that I didn't know as much as I thought I did, and neither did the mental health community.

A couple of years ago, I believed my manuscript was finished, and I got it formatted to self-publish. But it wasn't time. I got heavily triggered in marketing it, so it was back to the inner delving I went. It was when an editor looked at this current manuscript for the fifth time that I realized that the book needed to be divided into two volumes. The first volume consists mostly of references and reflections I have learned along the way; this second volume is a more personalized journaling that took those references and went deeper into the self than anyone has ever gone.

Within these reflections, God gave me insights into new revelations to serve us on our personal journeys to resurrecting love.

1
MY PHILOSOPHICAL JOURNEY

WHAT ATTENTION WAS I CRYING out for when I turned to drinking, stealing, running away, and sex?

Why did I only get my period once a year, if that? Why did my breasts start developing so early? And why didn't I grow taller than my parents? It was as if my body had stopped growing when it shouldn't have.

Why did every boyfriend cheat on me? And why would my best friend, at the time, sleep with the father of my son?

Why would I come home from work and crash on the couch, unable to emotionally care for my young children?

Why did I have a screen up to my husband, allowing in just so much care and love, while being suspicious of his behavior and attitude toward me?

Why did I have few trusted friends? Upon further inquiry, why did I choose some friends who treated me like my mother did?

Why did certain leaders and coordinators of my learning and working disrespect me, treat me unfairly, or ignore my efforts?

Out of desperation for answers and a new way, I kept searching until the way was shown to me.

2

CHILDHOOD

I AM THE OLDEST AND only daughter, alongside three brothers.

Self-inquire: being female, I am a burden. I am useless, incapable, and inferior to the male presence. I lack common sense, as I can't do what is expected of me. I cannot be what is demanded of me, and I persecute myself for that fact. I lose my sense of individuality, which takes away the ability to make a connection with self-worth. This creates shame of not fitting in as me. I escape trying to be me, as being me doesn't work.

My whole life has been colored with conflicted feelings for the maternal force in my life. I have experienced large doses of frustrated love, mixed with the heaviness of unbridled hatred. I learned to turn my hatred inward and participate in activities that could potentially hurt me as a way to escape my reality.

For many years, I did not understand what I was going through. I tried to rationalize it. I tried to understand life from Mom's point of view. I tried to please her. A comment of lack from her, and I would try to fix it. One of my few recollections of childhood is of me sitting on my bed after a tiff with her, and her saying, "If only you would … I could love you." My whole life has been about my need to be someone other than me, to get noticed in a positive way.

I am asleep to how I am affected by being a nobody. I feel secure, though, with her ignoring me.

I hold a mind-set of being fundamentally flawed.

I could finally put a word around my struggle of being me around my maternal influence: condescending—"having or showing a feeling of patronizing superiority"—with underlying envy.

I could never be okay with being me. I was told that I made up stories. I was unbelievably confused as to what was real and what wasn't. I grew up with huge distortions about myself and about love and support. I compartmentalized all aspects of my life, never feeling as though my life was one piece; I was fragmented.

I learned to close down to my feelings in my body and my emotions. I didn't allow my anger to rise because it wasn't allowed to be voiced, and I didn't allow myself to feel it internally, as Mom could sense that and punish me for it. I did express it externally, in the form of my behavior.

I physically hurt myself and got into fights, one time coming home with a bitten-out piece of flesh hanging from my arm. I was kicked out of high school twice, so I started working and volunteering at age fifteen. I ran away to sleep in a trailer that I broke into by myself, after a night of drugs. Police picked me up. I drank and was told that I was an alcoholic by an intake worker. I stole from people. I shoplifted. I sneaked out at night to jump the trains. I was pressured into sexual intercourse in my early teens. All these behaviors were a cry for someone to notice me and pay attention to me, regardless of the potential consequences.

Through my struggles, my body protected itself. My breasts grew large early, and I believe it was my body's way of protecting my heart. I never had my period—stunned the heck out of me when I was pronounced pregnant. My muscles were so tight, holding on to all the emotional suffering I hadn't released. Later in life, I experienced a lot of chest (heart) tightness, lower-back pain, digestive discomfort and pain, and the diagnosis of high blood pressure at age forty-nine.

Unraveling my childhood script to heal started in college, when I attended the Child and Youth Worker program. Such introspective work, and when the subject of shame came along, I knew that I'd hit a deep wound of pain and struggle.

I was told that I had to attend counseling because I couldn't hope to help someone else if I didn't help myself first. At home, I did so much journaling, crying, and letter-writing (never sending them). The healing started, but a wet blanket of depression stayed over me.

A friend told me about a course in 2007 that I had to attend. It gave me shivers as she talked about it. I had one week to register.

This workshop changed my life. (I apologize as I can't find this workshop online- I don't recall the name of it. My intention is to give you more than what I learned in this course.)

Through cathartic breathing exercises, I released emotional pain in my body that I was not aware of having.

As I lay on my back on the floor, I was instructed to breathe rapidly through my open mouth to the loud tempo playing in the background. My mouth got dry, but I had to keep breathing.

Soon, I felt tingling in my feet, and then the energy moved up to my knees and stopped. I tried to shift my body, as it hurt so badly. Then the energy rose to my hips. I ground my hips into the floor to try to ease the pain but without release, as the energy rose again to my chest and stopped. Again, I tried to grind the pain away but to no relief. This hurt more than all my pregnancies combined (and I was in great pain and had excessive bleeding with my daughter).

I started to cry.

Workers came to surround me and rub my legs, and they started to shake. Someone whispered in my ear to keep breathing. I cried harder. I cried so hard until the crying turned into a laugh. Then the pain was gone. The music stopped.

During reflection time, someone asked what that experience had felt like. I said that it felt like I was let free from being captive in the lonely, dark, wet basement.

I felt lighter and responded more lovingly toward my family when I got home. But depression still hung over me.

I took a course to learn Qigong. I incorporated that practice into my habits. During a reflection, a voice in my head gave me a name to call up. I had no clue what it was but upon searching online, I discovered it was a wellness/healing establishment. I had a Reiki session in 2011, in which the Reiki practitioner felt my thirteen-year-old presence hurting in my abdomen. She asked if something had happened at that age.

I said, "Yes. My mom said she was leaving, taking the boys, and leaving me with my dad."

I cried so hard afterward. I went back to one of the gatherings at the healing centre. I was triggered, and on my car ride home, I bawled until I laughed. A deep release happened again.

I now knew, through experience, that my body was hanging on to a lot of hurtful stories; sitting at the core was anger representing injustice at not measuring up. I denied the stories' existence, but the pain and tightness told me to wake up. I had some healing to do. Once I released some of that disruptive energy, I reacted differently toward my environment. I led with less hostility. I started to pay closer attention to what was put in front of me. I opened the doors that I wanted opened, and I walked through them.

Over time, I replaced my destructive behaviors with some serious self-care.

Yet, I still struggled!

Why was there this indefinite struggle?

I went to a women's retreat, where I was taught the basics of muscle testing, which is a unique way of accessing the body's knowledge of itself.

I started with getting a clear yes and a clear no, as I didn't trust myself. I was suspicious of whether my body would give me the truth.

I moved onward to uncovering my blocked emotions and the defense mechanisms I used to keep my beliefs intact, by tapping into the subconscious mind.

It only took a few months to release myself from the heaviness of the wet blanket, yet I was still emotionally and psychologically struggling. I experienced the effects as disconnection from intimacy with my husband, friends, and children. Plus, I couldn't move forward with any projects I had lined up, as I sabotaged the result with a mind-set of my bringing a bigger burden to success. I didn't know how to free myself from this energy.

Moving forward in life, I lacked a positive and true sense of self because there was no definitive Athena; I was not whole.

There was no acknowledgment of my femininity.

I saw myself as inferior to males.

Inferiority is the influence that causes one to assume the worst of self.

Inferiority plays out as putting yourself last, being self-less, ignoring your own needs, playing small, ignoring your emotions—basically, not giving yourself the respectful consideration you deserve.

I appeared as "less real." In ways, I did not exist. I was a projection of a reality of being inferior.

In numbness, self-importance digresses, as I am excluded from reality and from qualification (allowing space to set value on the importance of my essence showing up).

Not only am I excluded from my family's reality, but I am forbidden to form my own reality, which leaves me persecuted, which represents being on the outside, forbidden to fit in.

This hard lesson of being ignored enslaves me to servitude to establish a sense of fitting in.

Servitude represents doing for others before thy self and holding value for others before thy self.

I bring a bigger burden to life when the real me shows up, as I am a mistake.

Mistake represents a projection of scattered existence.

Within this projection, I describe myself as inferior, as I don't meet the standards for inclusion. A lack of emotional connection inhibits me from existing and showing up.

Follow-through becomes a focus on the futility of being good enough to measure up to the reality of subjectivity.

It establishes a focus on a power struggle for a connection with love, as love has been silenced.

This sets me on a life course of servitude to form an attachment to pretending to be something I am not (important).

The journey back to me became about the focus on proving that I exist and holding value as I am.

There was no encouraging connection to a subjectively (within) positive view of self, as I only learned to objectively (outside) connect to a distorted sense of self.

I was disconnected on every level of my being.

From my lack of nurturing, I learned to distrust women and give my power away to men.

My journey was to release myself from the trauma of being a mistake, to associate myself with being enough.

I was talking to my dear friend about what this process could do, and she offered me a name to use that would integrate all aspects; Wise Core Consulting was born.

The more I asked why, the more I learned about the effects of trauma and how we cope.

In the process of releasing from the identity I believed I was, I then had to rediscover who I was and what I could expect from myself and for myself. I had mind-sets and emotional tendencies that needed to be reestablished. Yes, the technique could do this!

I realized there were workshops I wanted to do when I went to a full-day conference to celebrate women in business. Halfway through, I fainted and vomited all over myself. I was brought to the emergency room by ambulance. They said my blood pressure was too high, and they had to figure out what was causing it. I knew that I'd thrown up and spiked my blood pressure by talking about myself and what I hoped to do. I felt my cheeks burn and energy rise in the anxiety of putting myself out there.

Following this incident, my intuition came on stronger, and my learning curve dramatically improved.

More chest, neck, and head pains came upon me. I slowly uncovered what the diagnosis was to the anxiety attack I'd encountered over the course of my journey here.

Meaning of depression: It associates with assuming the worst of my own reality.

Meaning of anxiety: In one word, *persecution* and expecting it of myself and/or from others.

It associates with constricting the importance to knowing I am whole in the regard of other's assuming the worst of me.

This was the most difficult five years of my life. I felt broken, like Humpty Dumpty, and as such, I didn't know how to put myself together. But I kept striving for answers. Thank goodness I had Wise Core Consulting and then the developing of my intuition to support this development of self. I will share with you a deeply personal version of what it took to free me.

3

AWKWARDNESS

I WAS SHARING WITH MY husband a few things about a new person I was getting to know. I said there was something about this friend that intrigued me, but I couldn't figure out what it was. I saw it as this person being different—but how?

My husband said the friend would be considered "socially awkward," just as he would be and our daughter claims herself to be.

I said that others would not think of me as socially awkward, but after more thought, I realized that I am extremely awkward. It goes hand in hand with feeling inferior. The word *awkward*, however, has never come to my mind.

And then it hit me: I was attracted to that part of my husband, as I felt safe in that essence. Unconsciously, I saw myself as a misfit in the family and in society, and that had me follow through as socially awkward, bordering on socially inept—something I have always tried to hide from, but how could I hide from myself?

I looked up *socially awkward* on Wikipedia and found its meaning is "to cause distress." I looked up distress: "suffering; misfortune; state of danger or great need." I always feel like I am in distress.

I can tell I hold back, drag my feet when I do go forward, and don't allow myself to fully let go until I feel totally safe in what I am doing. If I perceive any disappointment coming my way, I shut myself down. I don't trust my friendships—who is genuine and who is not toward me.

I believe that being genuine means that I am to assume the worst of my ability to bring in support that will create healthy friendships because I shouldn't believe that people want to nurture assuming the best of me engaging in connection with them.

I stay away from those who assume the best of my efforts of friendship. Instead, I gravitate to those who seem to damage my efforts. But if I am honest, they don't damage my efforts; it's really about my feeling like I don't fit in, and I assume it's because they don't think well of me, that they don't like me, and that I have nothing to offer to them. The truth is, the support of others afflicts me in belonging, as this creates a conflict within, as support and nurture have been about giving and not receiving. What I have received is that "I am not good enough to fit in and belong."

When I ask myself if someone is genuine, what I really want to know is if I can trust that person's influence to establish my existence as being on the inside.

Being in a relationship with myself, I bring myself down to influence assuming the best of inferiority over importance.

Ding. Ding. Ding. I get it!

I have been searching out there for a sense of being on the inside, when the inside has always been inside of me.

Wherever I am, I am on the inside—literally. I belong to me. Nobody owns me and my inside of belonging. I am love. My being is love. And in this love, there is nothing to prove.

To bring this new awareness to a deeper level, I remembered hearing about the eighty/twenty rule, which looks like 10 percent, 40 percent/40 percent, 10 percent.

This is how it plays out:

The first 10 percent will never be happy in life or content with me, no matter what I do.

The next 40 percent is the group that is unhappy but will change if it's beneficial to them.

On the other half, that 40 percent is happy, with some stress that affects living.

And the other 10 percent are always content, no matter what happens.

Most of us focus on the 10 percent that will never be happy and will never like us.

It would be beneficial to focus on the first 40 percent to bring them over to the next 40 percent and instill in them trust and belief in us and our influence to create a give-and-take relationship.

And it struck me: I pay too much attention to the 10 percent that I can never make happy.

When I perceive someone attacking me by assuming the worst of my reality, it instinctively triggers a survival focus on assuming the worst of my existence, which has me then out to prove I am genuine. I am always nice and calm in conflict to support my sense of being in existence, but inside, I instinctively want to advocate for the inner child who had to repress her emotions and just yell. Yell what? I start to cry.

Own it, Athena. Voice it. Yell it. *Fuck you!* I fucking hate you!

You tear me down by treating me less than. I allow this perceived 10 percent to dictate to me whether I am equal and if others view me as equal.

I go into my life, serving myself as disapproval.

I have a warped sense of what is right and what is wrong in me if I want to belong, be loved, and be a loving presence with my family, which bleeds out to the community. Lovingly expressing myself is wrong; I shut down. Sadness takes over.

I don't feel safe, as essence was restricted in being recognized as love.

My thread: The interconnectedness of the male and female influencing my existence has me impact women, damaging my importance, while men reinforce the damage. Women assume the worst of me, and men undervalue me.

Moving forward, any love coming my way could not be seen in my view that has had no previous attaching to consciousness of it. I would numb myself to it, in conflict of it. I didn't know how to handle it, so I assumed that what I learned in childhood was true in the moment, and I projected these influences onto those who tried to love me.

My husband loves me, yet I don't trust it. My sons love me, yet I perceive indifference from them. My friends like me, yet I am suspicious of their regard for me.

I expect to be judged. I hold a sense of injustice toward my past, so I don't allow my family to be released from that judgment of blame, nor do I allow myself to let go and move on. I sit in the heaviness of the effects of defensive judgment.

I don't have the ability to act as though I am real, as I was deprived of being acknowledged because of it. I have buried the scars of being deprived of family, but they sure are controlling my life.

Self-preservation: I am protecting my essence from being traumatized.

Innocence is lost in addictions.

In addictions, such as drug or alcohol use and prostitution, the signs of self-harm and self-hate are usually visible. But I never succumbed to either, and I keep wondering why I didn't, as I struggle with the same inner fight. I am literally divided in two.

To the outside world, people tell me I appear confident and sure of myself. When they get to know me, though, they see my insecurities come out. The fact that I haven't become addicted to outside destructive influences causes me to look competent, but on the inside, the split mind exists. The addiction of an inward destruction is a shutting down to self-love, which constricts any love coming in, which is devastating all the same.

My husband says that I keep going in a circle, which has me going deeper into the darkness of helplessness. I keep bringing myself down to attune with a family I see as suffering.

Commitment has meant traumatizing me to shut down a connection to loved ones.

4

EARNING MY KEEP

CHILDREN EARN THEIR KEEP BY following through on their chores, supporting their siblings on their journey, and forming strong, caring bonds with their parents by being open, honest, and trustworthy. The flow is a give-and-take of support for each other. They all feel equal and important, as they are encouraged to express their individual dreams, aspirations, and ways of doing things.

As a child, I was deficient in love and in the support of my basic need of having my everyday efforts seen as important and valued, and that caused me to set out into the larger world to prove my importance was valued. I strove to make my mark on the world before I learned to earn my keep by being me. I sabotaged making my mark as I learned that I wasn't okay by earning my keep being me. I work hard at getting myself out there before establishing a foundation of being me.

Earning my keep becomes a power struggle for an intentional childlike state of attaching to proving me important to keep. As I couldn't earn my keep, damaged importance caused me to try to earn my keep by following through on objectivity's importance to form me as a special purpose (look what I can do for you!). I searched outside of the whole to prove I was important enough to associate with and important and valued enough to keep.

My life, making a difference: will people feel certain of finding something to like about me, and will they want me in their circle? Even though my life hadn't made a difference with me in it, I didn't think I felt helpless. I tried to take control of my life. My set point didn't allow my life to make a difference, as it was shown to me that having the real self show up did not make a difference.

I am going to digress and share a frustration I have heard in different circles. There is an issue of workers not keeping the work vehicles and staff room clean; plus, keys are missing when they should be returned. I mention that everyone has their own sense of right and wrong, good enough or lacking, set point and upper ceiling, all based on what value means to them.

I digress from following through with my life making a difference. Paradox: value grows the more I shut down self-importance.

5

WOMEN

I HAVE NOTICED THAT A lot of us have learned to give of ourselves before we consider our own wants and needs, all in good favor of being nice and helpful. We are looked upon more fondly when we act modest and selfless, rather than important, because we have been misled to believe that it is sinful and selfish to think of ourselves as important, equal, and significant.

But as I taught in one of my workshops, being assertive, rather than passive or domineering, in your life and in your relationships with others starts with taking ownership of your stuff. As you stand in your power, hold respect for your opinions and perspectives, and take responsibility for your assumptions, you can speak up when you feel like someone has stepped over a boundary you have for yourself.

You aren't being mean or starting a conflict by speaking up for yourself; you are taking a stand for governing your own importance. And by taking a stand for your importance, you mirror to others that it is their right to do the same for themselves. It becomes a win/win situation, as you both are respected and regarded as independent, with your own minds and your own voices. It demonstrates freedom from external control or influence. When you stand in your power of autonomy to subjectively exist, you have nothing to prove and nothing to earn. You know you belong just as you are. There are no false pretenses; you are natural in your relationships.

And don't we all deserve the right to be true to ourselves?

If the answer rings *no* in your head, where is that prejudice coming from?

And yes, it seems like I am still struggling with owning my value.

6

MEN

THE FOLLOWING INSIGHT INFORMS ME of my struggle with men.

It's valid that I say I lack support from men, and I judge them as a firmness of intention of using me (mostly for sexual pleasure). Sexual pleasure represents providing men with existence. I laughed when this came up because my husband says that he feels most important when he's in bed with me.

But have I learned to see me as separate from the man? No. Has society reinforced the man as superior? I believe so. Am I the only one to believe this? No. Have we experienced value being highly regarded by the male? For the most part, women believe the answer is yes. Do men think otherwise? Those I have talked with have said yes.

But if I go deeper into the conversation, I hear that the men have been deceived as to what equality, respect, and value really mean. They are unsure of what it truly takes to hold a woman in high regard. They believe they lose manhood by doing so. Some of the stuff that comes out of young males' mouths astounds me. The ignorance of women's rights is so apparent. I hear the music the youth play. I hear the podcasts they listen to. There is an influx of a lack of value for specific groups, from women to Natives to Muslims in what is being proclaimed and assaulted.

Words matter. Actions toward others matter. No one life is more valuable than any other. Period.

POVERTY

I WENT TO A LOCAL talk on the core issues of poverty. As I was driving home, it hit me that I have a deep-set mind-set of poverty. If my husband didn't provide for me, I would be desperate to have my and my children's needs met. My husband once lost his job for a short time, and we had to apply for geared-to-income housing through the city. As a family of five, we survived on $15,000 that year. I don't know how we paid our bills, kept our car on the road, put food on the table, or bought our baby's medicine, but we were provided for.

When I have a job, I am uncomfortable making the money or asking for the money.

I am poor, mentally and emotionally.

This became a childlike state of attachment.

Survival became an innate process of self-denial.

This is what comes up next: We need to let go of assuming the worst of putting ourselves out there through our judgments, proving ourselves significant, our defenses, and our limiting reactions.

Until we can feel still and secure in our importance, we will never feel that we belong, fit in, are accepted, and liked for who we are and what we can contribute. Our power to be is not in changing something outside of us but rather in changing our perceptions, assumptions, and ways of being that keep us down in our own self-criticisms. We feel morally bound to stay loyal to the objective presence, while disregarding our needs and potential contributions. (To be fair, it isn't just women who deal with inferiority, abuse, neglect, and blindness.)

Morally bound represents that we overcompensate for a paradigm of inferiority, as we associate it with proving our worth or existence. Earning our keep reconciles following through with inferiority, as we are obligated to compromise subjectivity's existence, all in the name of love.

But I have to accept there is dogma out there proclaiming itself the truth. I can be sure that most of it isn't, as it distresses those who redirect the negativity of its message. Those who redirect are challenged, put down, called racist, and sometimes raped or killed because of their efforts to stand up to the competence of restrictive dogma having the upper hand. The negativity of certain dogma is competent in leading the way in redirecting love to becoming invisible, so that dogma and its leaders can become king of the jungle. More of us need to interconnect together to make love competent in leading the way as the truth for humanity.

8

SELF-IMPORTANCE AS AN INHERITED, CONCEPTUAL PARADIGM

DOES THE MODELING OF IMPORTANCE tear you down as shown in A (below), or does it bring you up and move you forward, as shown in B?

A. Self-importance as an inherited, conceptual paradigm of assuming the best of how an individual proves it exists as important and valued. (You have something to prove.)

This is an obligation of following through with inferiority for a gradation of earning one's keep (to exist as constricted importance) through overcompensating.

B. Self-importance as an inherited, conceptual paradigm of being prideful of following through with existing, as subjective attachment of proof with importance. (I have nothing to prove.)

This is a gradation of establishing assuming the best of contributing to follow through with nurturing an individual's expression of significance as the real self blossoms.

Are you conscious or unconscious of this inherited conceptual paradigm of importance?

A lot of people do not realize that they are struggling as their experiences have become their reality of truth. A lot of people do not reach out for support, as they were taught that their needs come last or that they aren't important.

Others have a fear of the unknown that sabotages them from following through on importance. Most hold a mind-set of futility, as they learned that this is how things are, and don't expect it to change.

And others protect a way of being so there is resistance to acknowledging an imbalance within and with their loved ones.

I was the person who felt heavy in mind and body, yet I had no clue that I was struggling in any way. I was oblivious to what my reality was. I was numb. But I was surviving and trying my best to live more congruent to me. Yet I felt like I had failed miserably.

I was extremely unconscious of my trauma, which had me a slave to seeing the world in one way.

One way you can tell if you are trapped by futility is if you try hard to gain success in something important to you, but you just can't gain momentum to get the results you truly desire. You can see some gain, and you try even harder to move to the next level, but something just doesn't give.

How many talented artists do we see strive but never get to the spotlight, or if they do, they sabotage their stay in the spotlight, and we wonder why, as they have so much talent?

How about the politicians who have a solid foundation of ethics yet are never really heard or seen as important in value, and we see the less-than-qualified get into power?

How is it that some children get support, with teachers engaging in their learning, resources, and chances to join in activities so easily, while others struggle to get to school and do well in learning?

A big part of it has to do with the modelling of importance to which they have adhered. Has it brought them up, or has it kept them down?

If you aren't aligning with self-importance, then with what are you aligning?

The truth is that we are all born perfect in the consciousness's reality. When we question our innate innocence, we step away from knowing to now proving our importance, which has us undermine the positives about us.

It is time for us to get back to the truth of who we are at the core—innocence.

There is no such thing as proving importance, as we are all born important.

And we don't need to work at belonging, as we are born belonging to life.

9

RECOGNIZING POSITIVE ATTACHMENT

I DO NOT RECOGNIZE THE positive influences I make. I believe I am creating a negative influence, but I do not realize the extent of it yet.

Most of us shift away from reinforcing bringing ourselves forward as we truly are. Why do we believe the power out there is more important than our actual importance? And why do we give ourselves over to that (Hitler, corrupt leaders, corporations and churches, family, addictions)?

First, I would say that the eyes of history allow us to collect all the data and then pull out the truth to learn from what has happened. Hitler did make positive headway with his country, but there were only a few who knew the real mind of what Hitler was working toward. He was deceitful and manipulative in his dealings with his people, which is hard to discern in the moment that it is happening, when we think it is all good around us. But I think that times like that would have us more aware in the presence of negativity, which is obnoxious and selfish in its deployment of standards to serve and live by, yet it seems that we are more asleep to it than ever.

Second, we often let go of regarding autonomy as having value, as it has created a competition with the outside for importance. (We have learned that we are less important than someone else, who seems to be more important.) We lost the competition, as we assumed the worst of our value. This has us assume the best of inferiority, as the objective way damaged any chance of getting back self-importance.

Their way (objective) has the power, as we assume the worst of our way, following through with aligning ourselves to a reality of value. Our follow-through of equality ignites a power struggle, as they want us to support them, and we want them to regard us as equal.

We have come to believe that the influence of control has more power than the influence of knowing autonomy of equality.

This is a historical, transgenerational transmission of trauma that cannot be traced to a specific undoing of influencing the importance of equality, yet it is experienced through a specific undoing of power (e.g., Natives taken over by settlers; Uganda genocide in 1971; Hitler's inner circle of Nazi leaders seize control of Germany).

Resilience patterns were insidiously undermined by the magnifying of conceptual power of importance—their way is more important than our way—which allowed for weakness patterns and the disease of attaching to objectivity's importance to become the autonomy of personal power.

As we assume the worst of self-importance in the need to fit in, we pretend to be important by establishing equality as proving an attachment to (1) forbidding the earning of equality, and (2) assuming the best of bullying.

Competition represents the death of subjectivity being real. They don't see, hear, or view us as being of value; they can only regard us as being inferior. If we are to challenge them on this, we can expect our reputations to be damaged.

We stay in a state of addictive self-shaming, instead of assuming the best of restoring self-importance. This is a learned helplessness of shifting away from taking responsibility for being accountable to claim or not to claim personal power.

Note: I couldn't bring this up on my own. I had my husband help me, as a modeling of a trait of inferiority prevented me from forming an opinion on the constricting of self-importance, which leads to addictive self-shaming.

The idea of self-shaming came from this: "I am being selfish/narcissistic by believing I am the Queen Pin of *everything*."

This has me identify as the problem in a negative, self-fulfilling narcissism of self-deprecation.

No wonder I am always suffering. No wonder it comes up, as I forbid—thus, reject—any love's expression through belonging in a relationship. No wonder I put all the attention on me and fixing what I believe is broken about me. How exhausting. How utterly alone I feel in this state. How narcissistic of me to put all the focus on me.

I am done with that!

A thought to ponder: Do you do any of the following:

- Compete for superiority (being on top)?
- Assume the best of your efforts to overachieve?
- Put up with repressing self-care (meaning that you go, go, and go but don't take the necessary steps needed for self-care)?
- Diminish the need for intimate attachments?
- Have an all-or-nothing attitude?

I will no longer wear self-deprivation as a badge for living.

10

EVERYTHING IS ENERGY

ENERGY PORTRAYS AS NEGATIVITY OR positivity. We can exist in a paradigm of variables distressed in negativity, or live in a paradigm of variables attuned to positivity, or reside in a paradigm of a power struggle between the two.

I noticed that no one was getting back to me about doing workshops. I could not recognize the intention I hoped to commit to in my presentations, and I was not progressing any further ahead. There was a block. I asked myself, "What am I not willing to recognize?" Then it hit me that I'd stated my intentions in the *negative form*—don't instead of do, can't instead of can, won't instead of will.

So I changed it to, "What do I need to recognize for myself?"

I need to recognize that I reinforce the negative instead of the positive to nurture the support of futility in feeling like me.

Trauma creates psychological change.

Nothing can get us back to where we wish we could go back to. Some of us feel like we have lost so much time and effort in getting to know ourselves on a real level. It feels sad, empty, and lonely. But coming through the trauma often brings about new characteristics and attributes of strength, compassion, caring, patience, tolerance, and acceptance.

You will never be who you imagine you could have been, but you can be someone so much more confident and competent in what you have gained. Bring all your learnings together, and use them to propel you forward in a mission that will feed your soul.

I feel so emotional that I know something has to come up.

Abandoning the wholeness of self proves the importance of family/ objectivity being more real.

This has been my life's story.

First, I try to fix people before I can move forward into my own sense of self, but the truth is, I cannot fix people. Second, I give up on me living so that others will be surer of themselves around me.

Yes, I am unknowingly influencing the scars of my past, just as most of us are. Our stressors of today are manifestations of unresolved stuff of yesterday. Our way of responding has just matured into manipulating our childhood coping mechanisms to either keep us back and staying small in our value or bringing us forward in a never-ending striving for purpose, as we believe we are ourselves in the space of distrust in being.

It is time to face that fact.

There is no hiding in value.

There always will be people who want to push us down and disable our value. We need to move away from being victims to the abuse of value by empowering our own realities of value.

Do not allow insults to stick to you. Rise above them.

It is not about being passive on boundary-setting with people, nor is it about being aggressive with who is to blame. It's about being assertive with being important—important in assuming the best of being equal. (We stand on the same ground, breathe the same air, and bleed the same color of blood.)

There is no hiding any longer from those who assume the worst of you. Own who you are, what you stand for, and what you contribute as value. Don't back down. Don't get your back up. Just *be*, in knowing your individual value is no less and no more than anyone else's value. There is no need to prove yourself worthy. There is no need to work at measuring up.

There is no point in arguing because you *know*. You know your value. You know others' value. In conflict, you know that it is a disregard of one's value that has them attacking the other's value. You know better. You now understand the conflict within.

What is up with white supremacy? I don't get it. Look at the pie charts of the distribution of the world population by color, and you will see that the white share is declining in numbers. The East is migrating to the West.

❦ ❦ ❦

I am in freeze mode.

I need a focus of feminine loving attention.

I want to lay my head on a robust woman's chest, and be wrapped in her embrace, and cry regret.

As I can't recognize love, connecting to love connects me to not seeing that people care about me.

I expect to be complete in being dearly loved, but I discourage it, acting out its significance because emotional flooding makes me incompetent at connecting to Beloved.

Flooding happens when intense feelings, thoughts, or sensations overwhelm one's ability to integrate them into the present moment. The system doesn't know what to do. One's ability to think clearly about the situation goes out the window, and a fight/flight/freeze reaction kicks in.

Victimhood commits me to invisibility.

What is the outcome to living invisible?

The outcome is living contrary to being satisfied with self.

We can see this denial of self in society's overuse of drugs, alcohol, sex, dieting, etc.

We are discouraging a clear yes to love interconnecting with our way of individuality.

How would you experience this?

You would experience an emotional flooding of helpless with regard to being overwhelmed by not being loved. Here are a few examples of how it plays out:

> Yield trusting others
> Discourage belonging
> Patronize Beloved
> Project that something is wrong with you
> Justify that people like you because they don't value themselves
> Act as if you can't outshine incompetence, so you stop trying
> Overthink
> Impact satisfaction as emotional flooding (who am I to be significant?), so you work hard, without stopping to enjoy the success
> Think you are only good to exert your value (people-please, codependency, overcompensate)

➢ Think you are a mistake at projecting love
➢ Resentment that offers no support
➢ Guilt for being loved
➢ Loathe that your love does not make a difference
➢ Emotional flood, as wanted, when love lacked
I see so many people comment on social media about the enduring heartache when a parent passes, knowing that they didn't get the love they needed from the parent when growing up. They compensate for abandoned love.

What's the answer?
Connect to Beloved—easy to say and hard to do.
Help!

11

LOYALTY/OBEDIENCE

LOYALTY/OBEDIENCE SHOULD NOT TRAP ME. Loyalty should not be demanding, expectant, and manipulative. I should not lose myself in the loyalty; that is codependence for existing as value. I should not have to partake in a power struggle to show loyalty; that is constricting each other's importance to prove one more worthy than the other.

I went out for a walk to get answers, and I came across a rock that was painted red with the words "Love at first sight" written on it. And it hit me.

Loyalty is what I feel with the love at first sight of seeing my babies. I want to protect them, feed them, nurture them, and love them. I will be loyal with always being there for my babies. But this is where I get tripped up.

At some point, loyalty becomes a liability, as I am obedient to the objective being value over the subjective, which makes me unsure if I am being smothering, nurturing, or bonding.

I am blocked.

I am blocked in believing that a soul tie supports me.

Soul tie of family? Yes. Soul tie of the collective? Yes. Is there a separation? No. Is there a separation of me in the physical to my team of the spiritual? No. Is there one from us to God? No and yes. We are of God, but God cannot attach if we imprint assuming the worst of the reality of being alive and love.

Note: We all influence, but people can be impacted only if they hold a clear no to positivity being whole. When they feel less than complete, they absorb the influence around them to try to make themselves complete. If they hold a clear yes to positivity, the influence becomes a consideration, not an attachment.

What is that space in between, detached from taking on influences and attached to be codependent on love?

It is being interconnected as complete.

I was talking to my husband about this recent revelation, and he asked me how I was doing. I didn't know. Indifferent? The words "I'm a void" came up.

The Void

How does this void get created? Let's start at the beginning.

What happens when the sperm meets the egg? The conception is an imprinting of love from the lower self or the higher self.

But what happens after the imprinting and before the delivery? By what is the baby being influenced as it grows and matures in the womb?

Baby is influenced either by assuming the best or assuming the worst of existing, as "love of the influence" gives a certain outcome of either a clear yes or a clear no to belonging as the real self.

Unconditional love is the only way to influence a clear yes to belonging.

I was imprinted with a clear no to belonging.

As I sat having breakfast with my husband, I could feel the warmth of my blood pressure rising from my chest. After breakfast, I went to snuggle, and a question came up: Why was I so comfortable in the dark with him the other evening, yet in the light, I get lightheaded?

It's about being visible in love.

I'm a threat to being significant being loved.

What is *love*? At this point, I am unsure of what love is. I went online to search, but I was unsure of what to search for. How did I get to *epigenetics*?

Epigenetics

Benedict Carey wrote in the *New York Times*:

> The idea is that trauma can leave a chemical mark on a person's genes which are passed down to subsequent

generations. The mark doesn't directly damage the gene; there's no mutation. Instead it alters the mechanism by which the gene is converted into functioning proteins, or expressed. The alteration isn't genetic. It's epigenetic.

The idea that we carry some biological trace of our ancestors' pain has a strong emotional appeal. It resonates with the feelings that arise when one views images of famine, war or slavery. And it seems to buttress psychodynamic narratives about trauma, and how its legacy can reverberate through families and down the ages. But for now, and for many scientists, the research in epigenetics falls well short of demonstrating that past human cruelties affect our physiology today, in any predictable or consistent way.[§]

Inquire: Epigenetics is the cause. It is an extreme denial of love that is imprinted from one generation to the next.

Assured of invisibility in love, existing makes no difference (why am I even here?), which makes for a depleted/deprived existence. This existence is filled with—there are so many words to describe it—heaviness, draining, sadness, grief, depression. I sit with it for a minute. My body hasn't admitted to this as of yet, but instincts tell me that the word I am looking for is *suffering*.

This suffering could have led me to suicide, prostitution, drugs, or alcohol but didn't. I had an important role that needed strength and determination. This role was to be the scapegoat, which ended with my taking on the responsibility of absorbing the suffering of everyone, mainly my family, which takes all the energy away from going out into the world as me.

It has kept me captive inside. But my body isn't ready to reveal the core to my suffering.

[§] Benedict Carey, "Can We really Inherit Trauma?" The *New York Times,* https://www.nytimes.com/2018/12/10/health/mind-epigenetics-genes.html.

12

EMBRYOS ARE MEANT TO BE COMPLETE AS LOVE

LOVE OF THE EMBRYOS CAN be marked with judgment, and not all judgment is the same. For me, the mark of judgment is committing to interconnecting presence with belonging, as there is no point because being love is marked by suffering. (We will give of ourselves but be deficient in the return of love.)

My youngest son opened up the next layer.

I was driving him to school, and halfway there, I acknowledged that I deprived him of his chance to play goalie when he was young, as I didn't recognize how he was in the zone. I apologized and said that we could put him back in, as it was never too late to put himself out there again.

He replied, "Yes, it is."

"Most people who played in the higher ranks are now playing in the men's league for fun," I said.

He replied, "It's too late. It's *go to the big leagues or go home*. I'm too old for the big leagues."

We arrived at the school, and he got out.

As I was driving home, I reflected on how it came to be that we only recognize ourselves as the opportunity to go to the big leagues, while diminishing ourselves in the given moment.

My oldest brother had natural skill at sports. When my kids were little, I took them to an indoor rink for a free skate, and my brother joined us. I was in awe of how smooth he was and the tricks that he could do on his skates. He was in the zone of competence and joy in that moment.

For a lot of people, presence in childhood was denied to be in the zone, radiating competence and joy in the freedom of self-expression. Just *being* meant suffering. You have to prove yourself big, but in a way, that made the parents proud or alive, instead of allowing yourself to feel good with being in the moment with presence.

It's been a heck of a long time since I've known what it feels like to just be content in expressing myself through artistic means. I am so unsure of feeling present in joy, with being able to express me in a fun, creative, and easy kind of way.

13

WHERE NEGATIVITY STARTED

NEGATIVITY IS THE ENERGY OF trapping the truth from being perceived as real.

Positivity is the existence of presence being love.

Love is a commitment to interconnect the self with the energy of living, which is the presence of love in form.

Why do women tend to bear and reproduce negativity?

The woman recognizes negativity as the way to mature love because of the man's commitment to encompassing negativity as the way to assert love.

Religion is the biggest culprit of keeping women invisible in being able to live true to their individual designs, due to men's commitment, which insists that the way of certain dogma is the truth of God; they use it to prove that this is how women should exist and be treated. Women will be subjected to suffering, all in the name of being disloyal to "the way" that keeps them trapped in subservience to the power of men's status/possession.

The man is blind to the real truth. He only can see what he believes is value if what he learned through his elders and the church is value—but is it truly value? He needs to truthfully ask himself this. And the woman has to ask herself if she is bound by dogma in the belief that it is normal and natural for her to be bound. But a woman has to feel safe to release herself from dogma that doesn't fit with her truth. Lots of times, dogma traps and beats down the woman for stepping out of the expectation set up by dogma.

14

FGM

THERE IS A WAY THAT is quite abusive to female rights. Consider an eight- or nine-year-old girl being pulled from school, as she is to get married to an older man, but not before getting circumcised, known as FGM.

Female genital mutilation (FGM) is, first and foremost, a violation of girls' and women's human rights. There is no developmental, religious, or health-related justification for the harmful practice. FGM is practiced in a variety of forms but is defined as "any procedure that involves partial or total removal of the external female genitalia, or other injury to the female genital organs for non-medical reasons."

Despite being a violation of girls' rights and prohibited by international law, FGM continues to be practiced in many countries because gender inequality and discriminatory social, cultural, and religious norms uphold the idea that FGM preserves chastity, cleanliness, and family honor. FGM is also linked to social norms regarding beauty and femininity.

Plan International perceives these beliefs to be rooted in a perceived need to control female sexuality. The ironic truth is that most often, it is women who circumcise their own as a practice that is revered as normal.

Normal is children denied rights and girls denied equality.[*]

Let's defy "normal" and support organizations that do.

UNICEF predicts that if there is no reduction in the practice of FGM between now and 2050, the number of girls mutilated each year will grow from 3.6 million in 2013 to 6.6 million in 2050.[**]

---

[*] FGM (Female Genital Mutilation), https://stories.plancanada.ca/ending-fgm-why-these-3-traditional-cutters-are-putting-down-their-knives.

[**] UNICEF, "Take Action to Eliminate Female Genital Mutilation by 2030," https://www.unicef.ca/en/press-release/take-action-eliminate-female-genital-mutilation-2030.

I would suggest watching a TEDx Talks on YouTube called "The Virginity Fraud" by Nina Dølvik Brochmann and Ellen Støkken, which that debunks myths with detecting female virginity—another way that controls females.

15

NURTURING SUPERIORITY

HELP! I AM ANXIOUS ABOUT giving my big speech tomorrow!

What about Athena?

Please notice me.

I just want my love to make a difference!

My Big Speech

My speech is tonight, and my mid-back is hurting. I am doing my breathing exercises but feel off. But when I am at the podium, I breathe and start. I flow. I am in my element.

The food is good, but I find I am eating to fill a void, as I can't feel satisfied for the success of tonight.

In the morning, I sit with it to see what comes up. I cannot celebrate, as I cannot feel satisfied with what I have done. I am punishing me. I have internalized that I am broken, so I undermine everything that I do.

In childhood, I anticipated punishment, and in adulthood, I anticipate punishment from me, which comes with the emotional flooding of *something is wrong with me.*

What have you taken on as truth or as a way of being, based on how you were treated?

Another aha hit me: if you have learned, as I have, that love is bad, unwelcomed, suspicious, undermining, neglectful, suppressing, disapproving, and incomplete, you would learn to scapegoat as disappointing meaning, you would identify and act out the opposite of what you are (love), to belong in a way that others need you to be (conditional), to pretend that you fit in.

You are disappointing, in that you are no longer living true to you, which feels damning. You can't forgive and move on if you feel damned. Love becomes closed off to you. Love becomes a distant memory. (Now I truly understand what being disappointing is.) Love becomes about separating from the whole of you to have part of you connected to others' reality of value, which is about the streams of inferiority. You perceive yourself as incomplete. You are living a lie.

With our value on the back burner, we align with efforts to reinforce servitude to others because we are trying to get our major needs met.

A woman called me up for help. She said she hadn't been diagnosed but had been looking online to search for her symptoms and found them under a few labels. I suggested she stop looking, as these symptoms only pointed out to her that labels imply she is flawed, incomplete, or a misfit. I told her to recognize the voice or energy as something outside of herself, not to judge or shame it but just to notice it and repeat, "This is not of me."

Breathe, and let any emotion rise.

What came up in thought?

I was getting ready to meet with a young woman to discuss an interview I wanted to do with her on a new television series I wanted to start through our local planning station. But my mid-back tightened up, and it was hard to breathe. When I did meet up with her, I was able to support her in how she saw herself in the big picture and how her breast cancer was telling her the many ways she put herself on the back burner and felt guilt when she tried to bring herself to the forefront.

Why is life so complicated?

It is complicated as we try to prove ourselves sovereign, but we tend to move away from ourselves.

When will we stop proving sovereignty? When we restore progressing being in tune with superiority of self by assuming the best of our reality as being of value.

My daughter phoned me while I was checking into this. She was having guy issues. She started to like them, and they really liked her, but then they disconnected from the relationship, which left my daughter confused as to what happened. I've encountered this several times. When I checked in, it said that this was an introjection of identifying with me, her mother, as shame. And what she was doing with these young lads was projecting that "my love doesn't make a difference," which was my influence.

I talked with my husband for his input, and he asked, "Why do you put your time into this type of guy?" Yes! We put our time, money, focus, care, and love into the negative people, who take but don't give back, while we turn our backs on the positive people who want to shower us with love. There is a lot of positivity out there, but are we attuned to it? No.

Sound familiar to you? Do you like the bad boys or jealous girls? I certainly did.

Are you trying to prove that you exist or earn your keep as being of value by constricting your efforts from mattering, so that you can serve others' agenda while ignoring your needs? It should be the other way around. They should be earning your respect and proving to you why it is in your best interest that you serve them. They shouldn't expect anything from you. You need to have expectations of them—and it takes time to unfold to see the progression of their sincerity toward you.

My husband keeps asking me how I rise above this self-sabotage, as I am learning a lot, but I am not moving forward.

My body keeps redirecting me. The focus is to be out there, not inside. That's why information for the collective keeps coming up.

Personal Style

> Style and self-esteem are innately connected.
> —Stacy London

I lack an identity that truly belongs to me.

I don't feel okay in my body or skin. I can't look in the mirror and see me, never mind liking what I see.

Ignoring me created an identity crisis and shame around my body, my looks, my self-expression, my style, my femininity, my desires, and my personal satisfaction. I lack proactivity and pride for what my body can do and has done (produced four babies).

Let Loose, Women

My husband has wondered why he loves my pink jacket so much. And then it hit him. He loved images of the 1960s, '70s, and even the '80s, as women wore color, burned their bras, and were sexually open in their expressions.

Then the '90s seemed to market grunge and black as the main color, while the early 2000s had women wearing padded bras. A friend took me to a sexy lingerie store to get my first padded bra. With this bra came the unconscious shame of my nipples showing. And sexual openness? Somehow, women were shamed and put back in their places of being seen in a certain light and treated in a certain way. It seemed that women were brainwashed to give themselves up to a way that was designed to hold them down or to hold them back from the light of self-expression.

Loss of Memory

I remember someone saying in an interview that she'd forgotten her twenties, as she was always wearing a mask. She was never authentically herself. That was my childhood. I was never authentically myself, and there was a lot of anxiousness with which to coexist, so why or how could I remember something (all my experiences were laced with being overwhelmed) or someone (I was suspicious of them) that existed to haunt me?

We won't form a memory when we are trying to zone out our existence, as it is too painful to do so; our minds shut down. Zoning out or escaping is a protection mode to try to escape that which causes us to fight, flee, or freeze.

Other's should not joke about our not having a good memory because there is trauma under there.

People have asked me why I don't like hot food. They've offered something to which I can give a response.

They said they "like the burn."

I said, "I don't like the burn."

They like the burn of pop going down the throat, but I don't. I don't like the burn of sore muscles. My intuition says that this relates to money too. I don't like the burn of making money. I didn't know there was such a thing! What does the burn represent?

The burn represents bitterness.

I am bitter at not being loved, which overwhelms me trying to be a somebody.

The root cause of bitterness is jealousy that hurts my reputation of being complete.

I am avoiding me. I am still running in circles.

I had my good friend over for coffee and freshly made cinnamon buns. We challenged and played off each other's wisdom.

I shared what had come up with me, and she said, "You aren't undermining. And it isn't nurture that you want from your mom."

I said, "I know! But what really needs to come up?"

She sat quietly for a moment and then said, "Athena, you are hoping to be seen, thinking that maybe this time, if you show yourself to her, it will be the time she notices you."

That resonated with me.

She said that she knew this inner child, as it was also her inner child that she tapped into.

I hoped to be seen as important, but each time I went to my mother, feeling assertive satisfaction with expressing self-significance, she slammed me down, treating me like I didn't belong, as everything about me was wrong.

And then I thought of the word *hope* and looked it up in the dictionary.

Hope is desire with the expectation of fulfillment. Hope is exactly what I have a barrier to. Desire was shut down, to expect anything good from happening for me and to me.

We can only have hope if we can see that we have a present and a future to go toward.

A lot of us are delayed in getting what we need, as we learned that our needs would not get satisfied. Delayed gratification comes from a lack of feeling secure in knowing that our needs will be met. And what is the need for me? My need is to feel safe in love.

Changing focus, I have heard from people in our conversations that most constitutional ties are patriarchal, as nature has dictated it to be so— nature or nurture? I believe that women have been attuned to the doctrine of the dominant ideology being patriarchy, but that doesn't make it true that we are not equal in existing as a reality of value.

But who says we are not equal in the patriarchal system? There is more than one perspective in any given situation. We can say that we see inequality in the behaviors put toward us, as actions speak louder than words. But are our interpretations coming from past trauma that sees us as being treated less than equal? And if so, would it change if we were to change, as the mirror wouldn't project that pain out to us any longer?

This is where the conflict lies in me. I am confused on what is right, what is wrong, and what is neither, as it's just a perspective and what is not of me but I assume it is.

My experience of the patriarchal leadership is of control by suppression. I don't want to fit in by conforming to the head of any individual or group who believes that their way is the way to being the authority over the affair of personal power. This way constricts my reality and my way of what it means to exist as being fully alive, complete in value, and in charge of my own affairs.

Being true in being ourselves is in the expression of our personal power, attuned to being complete in the masculine and the feminine, being equal in the existence of being real and genuine in value.

Once we start labeling everything, we show that we believe we are less than complete.

There are a lot of patriarchal (female and male) leaders in this world who believe that their way is the justified way to being a reality of value, but they have yet to realize how that way constricts follow-through of honorable service.

What Is the Focus?

The efforts of the feminine energy focus on the efforts of the masculine energy for a sense of being included in existing as value. There is a balance in the giving to receiving. The male energy provides the opportunity to move forward, while the feminine energy reinforces the efforts by engaging in the focus, details, and follow-through.

A lot of us have a hard time believing that we should trust in the masculine authority of progressing forward movement, as the belief of being inferior (not measuring up), held by the collective, conducts an attachment to the masculine as an undermining of assuming the best of us, existing as a duality in the reality of value.

And a lot of us ignore the feminine energy, as this energy reinforces bringing the masculine up by the feminine efforts, attaching as approval. In the movie *A Star Is Born*, the male character doesn't allow the progressing of approval by his beloved, so as to bring him up; he doesn't trust her being attached to him, as he doesn't see himself as being equal to her, so what is there to approve of? He conducts a misguiding of her believing in him, as he is considered undervalued. His love's manager/friend tells him that he is bringing down his beloved. He sabotages their love to undermine her efforts to bring him up in approval.

The anxious people have learned to expect backlash at influencing a belief in one's own truth, having never having the assumption that it would be contributed to with respect and honor in being equally different and unique. As a result, the anxious constrict progressing bringing themselves forward, as they focus on avoiding the indifference projected onto them, which represses aligning with restoring personal measuring up to value. Some people work hard at putting themselves out there but with anxious progressing of their truth, and it plays out as excluding existing as a structure of value.

I have seen women (and men, but men are conditioned to believe that this is their way) break down from over-running their masculine side. They get sick or hurt or pained in some way, as they are depleting the feminine nurturing of restoring balance.

Do you constrict the efforts to contribute in engaging in all truths, due to viewing yourself as the superior one? Would you be aware of this? No, because you would ignore the power struggle that it creates, as you try to have your reality be the valued one. This is patriarchal in nature.

Initiating the power struggle excludes the progress of assuming equality of value for the other person's reality. The anxious, being in the power struggle, constrict their reality to focus on progressing the two types of passive-aggressive realities as being of value, to belong on the inside, accepted as part of the valued.

The *passive assertives*—they say, "Trust me in leading you through my way"—contribute to constricting the nurturing of being approved of, as they have established themselves as a focus of being unbalanced (think of Bradley Cooper's character in *A Star Is Born*).

The *aggressives* constrict space of having the anxious be noticed in their way. The undermining of attuning with existing, as value in our younger years has us being the passively anxious ones, grabbing on to the aggressive contributors as love.

Our childhood was guided into assuming the best of their existence as the reality that should be valued. The aggressive leader is valued, as we approve of not being equal in their eyes, hoping for a focus from them to bring us up. We do not exist if they have not approved us into existence.

There is only one reality with a multitude of different and unique perspectives attuned as being of value. No one perspective is more worthy of attention and respect than another perspective.

But I resist nurturing my own power because I am being contrary.

Contrary: whatever someone projects on to me, I mirror back as an extension of it being about me.

Most people live contrary lives.

Example: I am unloved by others and am love to others. I am not special to others, and I am special to others. It can look like I project success, yet experience lack. I don't believe he is there for me, yet he expresses through his actions that I matter.

The mind of the objective consists of the lower self, ego, inferiority, constriction, obey, servitude, perception, assuming the worst.

The heart of the subjective consists of the higher self, superiority, the emotional body, assuming the best, a respective experience, being genuine.

The mind of the subjective consists of knowing the truth.

MANIFESTING

I AM CURIOUS HOW SOME leaders rise so quickly in their manifesting of money and influence. Does it have to do with a dimension, as I have been hearing about the fifth dimension, although I have no clue what it is.

Yes, part of the leader's success has to do with the fifth dimension.

Detached from believing in superiority constricts manifesting, which deprives a follow-through of the fifth dimension. This inherited sense of incomplete denies superiority access to the fifth dimension of manifestation.

I watched a video explaining the fifth dimension and realized that I am in the fifth dimension but constricted from contributing to attaching to being on the inside of the dimension, as my efforts aren't being taken as sincere.

In the fifth dimension, I am influenced through a lack of exercising control in regulating my behavior of bringing me forward. Bringing me forward is a modeling of self-importance, but I am anxious in attaching to this modeling.

Yet again, something is telling me to keep moving forward into inquiring.

A dream says it's a paradigm.

Expansion

I watched a YouTube video on "Five Signs You Are in the Fifth Dimension,"[††] and it hit me that I can't move forward, as I can't see the possibilities, as I lack the ability to expand on what it would look and feel like to move forward into my highest possibility.

[††] Diving Deep, Infinite Waters, "Five Signs You Are in the Fifth Dimension," https://www.youtube.com/watch?v=SkxF3MuDFww.

Of course! Constriction of being shut down and kept down depletes expansion!

I cannot expand if I cannot see that modeling pride is important, and if I cannot influence being attuned with pride, then I cannot see the value in me.

A paradigm of superiority includes pride for equality, happening through the establishment of an attachment, with modeling self-importance, due to being attuned as value.

I need to get my big-girl panties on and rebuild contributing to bringing me forward by establishing a belief that I can personally establish a sense of superiority, by assuming the best of influencing positive messages of being favored as the genuine one. People want to be around "real" people.

As one woman replied to one of my posts, "Athena is a super woman! I met her about 10 years ago at a workshop she was offering and she has been an indispensable resource and support for me since then. She knows how to bring people together in a way that allows everyone to shine their light."

Freedom happens when we choose to rebuild by sitting still long enough to hear the truth of who we are. We are love. We are loved. We are loving. The mind of the objective can have us think that the truth hurts, but it's in the repression of assuming the best for ourselves that we hurt and are unable to access the subjective reality to bring us, being whole, into the light of love.

Let's gather together that which we sowed to embrace the nourishment meant to bring us to complete living.

Assertive superiority is about being complete in being attuned with existing, as a reality of being imprinted positivity.

If you are not encompassing yourself within assertive superiority, you will find yourself

- constricting,
- lying,
- deceiving,
- depriving,

- restricting,
- repressing,
- ignoring,
- denying,
- anxiously detaching, or
- assuming the worst of some aspect of superiority (soul, spirit, mind, heart).

Reflect: How do you exclude yourself from attaching to loved ones?

Reflect: How do you exclude others from focusing on nurturing you?

You can only be attuned to love if you are attuned to attaching to support.

Reflect: How do you keep love to you? Do you push other people or opportunities away from your special love? Do you want this love all to yourself?

17

THE ADDICTIVE PERSONALITY

THERE IS A THEME IN the conversation going around our house, and it's about addictions. From musicians to family members who are addicted, my husband believes that making a decision to stay away from certain people will encourage them to stay clean and move on being healthy. I say that there can be more underlying and undermining themes for some people; that no matter how hard they try, they can't make therapy stick. They keep going farther down the rabbit hole. This addiction can be to drugs, food, pornography, sex, working out, or work. I am learning that there is so much more to what this all means and why we stay in the struggle.

Let's try to make more sense of it.

I believe that I am addicted to a certain way of being that keeps me trapped from playing big, which is living my life, my way, by my own rules.

I am learning to believe that our stress of "trauma drama" is an addiction to staying small, quiet, unseen, unheard, unvalued, and unequal.

What stress keeps recycling for you, and what is the play-out of it?

Stress, most often, is an outcome of unresolved trauma that keeps reinforcing its effects on our daily lives. We are so used to the effects, and most times, we are unaware of what caused it in the first place. It brings us down and holds us down. And we identify it as being a part of us on a personal level.

All helplessness represses restoring personal living to a functional mind-set of existing as a paradigm of love.

All negative stress has an addictive component to it.

An addictive personality controls the pain of avoiding—*what are you avoiding?* I have been avoiding the guilt of a play-out of being loved.

Even though my body keeps bringing up that I am shut down from restoring my way, I know that my family is not shutting me down, as they want me to get up and out! They do not stand in my way of self-efficacy. I block my way from being visible to let go of autonomy.

Why would I do that? Hmm. Ah! I get it! I don't shut me down, but to be visible, I have to shut me down to survive.

I am being counterproductive, meaning that I experience the opposite of the desired effect.

What is under all addiction? Is great suffering the reason why individuals need to escape from their reality?

I had two experiences in which I felt the overpowering draw to drink more. It was an *energy of invisibility,* trying to keep me hidden, that was committing me to connect to the need to have another drink. I have never succumbed to feeding this need because of my commitment to claiming positivity over the maturing of the negativity handed down to me.

It is this energy of invisibility that commits familial addiction and me to shutting down to love as a way to escape a reality. The reality is that being treated as invisible in love is depriving. It is painful to be treated as if something is wrong with our love and that we are wrong for being love.

We all wish to escape the pain of being deprived of love and loving. We are nothing if we cannot love.

Everything relates as love, closed to it, or being open to it.

Love is complete. Everything outside of love is incomplete.

BECOMING

THE EGG AND THE SPERM join together, complete in a primal mode of believing in its existence as love.

If the process of *becoming* is undermined, the embryo self-destructs in belonging, as there is no security of love of self as okay to nurture belonging. This is a denial of being love.

In denial, there is panic in being persecuted for recognizing the self as being authentic as love.

What is happening? What am I doing wrong? How am I wrong for living?

Helplessness is a gradual progression of repressing a mind-set of self-empowerment. If you do not feel safe in the womb, you are anxious to attach to the outside world, as you are helpless in trusting that you can assume the best of you and what is to come. An energy worker told me that I resisted leaving the womb. I believe that we know our destiny before we are conceived.

A power struggle to assume the best of the self comes into play—anxious attaching (lower self) vs. reinforcing assuming the best of being complete (higher self).

When the egg and the sperm meet, hereditary attachments influence the developing self. Are these influences positive or negative in nature?

Life Will Halt

I have to share with you that I cannot access the bar (what's it called?) on my computer that allows me to save or bold or print. At times, when something needs to come but doesn't want to, my pens won't work. When

I was at a weekend course for manifesting, all the new pens didn't work. I knew that anxious energy was causing it. We can easily influence the energy in so many ways if we do *not* want someone to do something specific or if we are fearful of a certain outcome.

My energy is still constricted. (*Own it, Athena!*) I am helpless! It is futile to set me free.

Am I focusing too much time on the mind? Yes. I intellectualize self.

I was not nurtured to attune with essence, so I recognize the truth— that I was born to adhere to the family's law as the way to live, love, and belong.

🦋 🦋 🦋

Sometimes, we are left feeling vulnerable to the unknown, as not having our feelings or needs taken into consideration leaves us feeling invisible in the decision-making that needs to occur.

A lot of grief, anger, or bitterness can come up, as the pain of being disregarded or cared for in the aftermath of loss can leave devastating effects on coping and moving forward in one's life.

Do you believe you have lost control of your ability to thrive and do well for yourself on your own?

Sometimes, we lose hope or lose sight that we will get that visibility/ care/regard back that has us living only for today. We feel alone. We feel lost. We feel abandoned. We don't understand what happened between having it and then its not being there. What did we miss?

Did we do something wrong? Self-blame pops up. We don't forgive ourselves easily. But what do we have to forgive? We are confused.

How has it played out for you?

Superiority is *living*, while judgment is *existing*.

Attuned to your higher self, you are a paradigm of superiority, living complete.

Attuned to the lower self, you are a paradigm of invisibility, existing in judgment of perceiving yourself as incomplete. Living is denied, as you try to prove you are visible and worthy of being.

19

A REFLECTION OF ME

I KEEP THINKING BACK TO an encounter I experienced a few months back. I was doing push-ups against a tree on the path I walk along the river. My head fit into the split of the trunks as I leaned in. I had finished and started walking again when I hear a loud *hi*. I looked back, saw a young girl, and said *hi* back. I kept walking, and again she yelled *hi*, more forcefully this time. I looked back and saw that she was running up to me. I was pleasantly surprised and asked her if she was nervous about talking to strangers.

No, of course she wasn't, and why would she be? We walked and talked until we got to the split in the road, where she went one way, and I went the other.

What did this grade-five girl have about her that made me think of her often? My husband said it's that she represents me. It's taken a few months to acknowledge how this girl reflects who I am, as I can see it arise in what has come up for me.

In the last month, I have been to a hot-weather destination for my eldest son's wedding and to the big city for my youngest son's sport tournament. In the airport, I complimented ladies, talked to the men, and had free-spirited conversations.

In the big city, with my youngest in tow, I talked to a young lad about where we live, and he said that he was going to attend school in our city. As he loved the same sport as my son, I thought he would get along with both my sons, so I invited this lad to dinner when he got to town in the fall. He excitedly accepted my invitation.

We have texted about our visit since then. I am thankful that my son saw this interaction, as it's not what he expects from me. At home, most of my interactions seem flat or insecure. Home depresses me. But I am learning why right here, right now.

Inquire: I am still in the effect of abuse.

I receive what I perceive.

To perceive means to become aware or conscious of (something); come to realize or understand.

And I perceive me as unlovable to soul tie. I am working on this, though.

20

BIPOLAR

I HAVE FRIENDS WHO HAVE been labeled as bipolar. Most refer to themselves as being bipolar, as it's a chemical deficiency in the brain that they will have for the rest of their lives. It's hereditary. It's a disease. That is what I am told. Instinct tells me, and then I confirm that it is a disease but not one that has a life-expectancy rate. It is not a chemical reaction that cannot be cured. It is labeled as such, as that is considered the truth (which is the disease), but it is not the truth, as you are learning through my journey to heal.

The system increases medication when bouts of depression knocks down individuals, but it doesn't do anything to raise them up. It doesn't do anything, as it isn't getting to the meaning of the depression. The body forces each person to wake up and take notice, while the medication forces them to keep it down.

I do not know why I haven't been labeled with a mental illness—as I learn the effects of other people's disorders, I see that I easily could have been. But then, I do not believe in being labeled, and I do not believe taking pills for certain "disorders."

A coworker said to me that I was not validating her struggle. I said I was validating her as a person, her struggles, and her value but was not validating that she was permanently bipolar, which was the story that she was hanging on to as her identity.

To Break It Down

This person is exceptionally strong, independent, competent, and capable but does not recognize this about herself with certainty. (Same here.)

She is attuned to not being good enough, broken, misfit. (Same here.)

She has a wall up to love.

Trauma happened in her childhood.

She is up and down in her moods, thoughts, and perceptions.

She was not nurtured into her own sense of self by Mom.

She does not know what unconditional love is. (The same for me.)

She is detached from personal and social love.

If she was to attach to love, life would be complete.

She is split in two. One part is strong, and the other part restricts love of self and love from others. If she would bring in that part, her life would normalize for the better.

Hmm. I still see me in this scenario. *Why?* Because all of us are not nurturing becoming more than the negativity of our childhood scripts.

> If love is unconditional acceptance, then we are living
> under the weight of conditional rejection.

I inquired into two people's meaning of bipolar, and it was judgment of committing to self being visible, as their roles needed to stay the same—that of building a parent/someone else up before self. I checked into a few others, and blame from early childhood was the culprit.

Everyone has his or her own meaning, although there can be a lot of similarities between the meanings of each person's mental health diagnosis. We all have our own lives to live and tell, but the core is the same: we are positively loved or not, and if we haven't been, we live out the effects.

I saw a sponsored ad on social media that showcased a popular therapist. I asked myself if her transformational program would be the one to help me, and the answer I received was yes.

I asked if I was discounting myself, and the answer was yes again. If I didn't discount, would I be the one with the information that could heal me? Yes.

I have been deprived of the right to define me and empower vitality toward making my life successful in its manifestation of self-significance.

I am trying to put an emotion to the mood I feel, and it's *agitation*. By putting myself out there, I trouble the mind of helplessness, as the effects of incomplete make me certain that I express as insignificant.

*   *   *

I went to bed and dreamed that I wanted to cheat on my husband.

After eating breakfast, I climbed back into bed with my husband, and he asked me how I was doing. I felt like a void so my reply was that I was numb. I am glad that I can recognize that state now. Then an uncontrollable emotion arose when we started to get intimate.

What is this uncontrollable emotion that comes up in intimacy?

It's acknowledging that I am engaging in lovestruck, identifying me as lovable.

This brings up deep sadness, which feels heavy as well as a validation of being unlovable that feels so tight in my body.

The mind feels disabled in acknowledging that I can empower soul-functioning dynamics within intimate connections with others.

Oh, my goodness! How this all plays out has really come alive in the past few days. It shows me that I haven't gotten to the core yet.

21

BEING INVALIDATED

WHAT IS REALLY BOTHERING ME is a sense of righteousness with concerns to abuse or trauma.

It's like, "I haven't been raped or done hard drugs or been to jail, so I haven't been traumatized."

I am confident and capable, so I couldn't be dealing with effects of neglect. I haven't dealt with bruises or lashes on my body, so I haven't been abused. This boy's mom doesn't do drugs, so he isn't harmed. This girl's mom puts clothes on her back and food in her belly, so she isn't neglected. There is this absence of recognizing the devastating effects of emotional and psychological abuse and neglect. Because there are no physical scars, the child/adult is okay and just has to get on with life.

I have been told all my life, "Athena, you're so cute" (meaning that because I am cute, I couldn't possibly have done some of the things I did). Or, "Athena, you just need to get over it and move on. Be positive. Be your confident self"—as if I'm purposefully depressing myself from believing that people actually want the best for me.

I wake up in the morning with a sore, tight mid-back. My heart hurts. And I am so sad. I do not know how to allow myself to see love in positivity.

Mixed messages create such confusion in my mind. I don't know what information I can trust and what I can dismiss. I don't know who I am and how I actually represent myself. I am only certain of negativity, and even in that, I question the validity of it. Positivity has had minimal, intentional focus in my life.

I am always muscle testing the questions, "Does my husband love me or not? Does he want the best for me?" If the answer comes up yes, then I second-guess and ask if the answer is the truth. If the answer is yes, then why do I feel like shit?

Do I leave, or do I stay? This question arises every few months for me. And then I wonder, *Why do I look at my son as though he is a bully to me?*

My youngest son and I have been in a power struggle for about eight years; that's how long we have been in this house. He seems to assume the worst of me.

Self-inquire: I don't perceive that I have the power to influence positive change.

My son was vulnerable in having to abandon all that he knew. In his vulnerability, he became uptight within the change that was happening. I took his behavior personally. I thought he wasn't paying attention to how I wanted to govern family through this change; he was the one being obstinate. But it was really me, overextending my childhood commitment to stay unconscious to how I actually relate with loved ones.

For me, the boundary of self has become the shadow. To break this down further, the boundary is a state of being in the shadow, where I am recognized as loyal to the lie. *What is the lie?*

I am marked by denial and invisibility as well having the light and the shadow validation reversed, which creates a judgmental mind, plus a body that is persistent in denying progress of becoming visible, out of a commitment to support negativity as the truth.

I've asked people I know to support me by reading my book but have received mixed messages.

Why would hopeful support be afraid of helping me?

People are afraid of bringing me on the inside, as they feel they have been betrayed by the governing of someone else's self-importance at another time.

Ah. Good to know.

How ironic that this came up, though, because after I typed this, I went for a walk with a leader who has had a lot of training to work with North American Indians (a woman elder told me that they like the name *Indian*). She mentioned that their not looking at us (*us*, as privileged white people) in the eye is supposedly a sign of respect for us, and their holding back from being in the spotlight is about humility. But after all this uncovering of the truth, I will challenge those notions.

What if it is all learned behavior to self-protect over time? How would a generation and then the following generation, through influence, learn to express or communicate, when the white settler, after some time, rebuked their ways and stopped looking to them for solutions? When disrespect, inferiority, and captivity came into play, how would the Indians stand up to that? How did the Natives learn to handle this unequal balance of power?

Native American boarding schools, also known as Indian residential schools, were established in the United States and Canada during the late nineteenth and mid-twentieth centuries, with a primary objective of assimilating Native American children and youth into Euro-American culture. With eliminating the Native's traditional way of life, not only did a disempowering of equality and a disrespect for differences come into play, but a shutdown of Native identity took over. The Natives became anxious of the ignorance the white man had of how they reinforced the shut-down of the Native way while assuming the worst of their culture.

Equality and respect need to take an important place in the dealings with the Native tribes and peoples.

The Native community, as a whole, has not been subjected to dehumanizing trauma, but as a culture, all will be affected by the unresolved negative energy attached to each person's perspective of what he or she endured.

I have come across Natives who will not look me in the eye or acknowledge that I exist, while others look right at me, nod their heads, and address me in a positive way. What makes these interactions different is how each one perceives his or her world. Is the world safe? Can they assume the best of white people? If they stand up for their rights, will they be respected as equal in consideration of importance? Do they matter? Will what they contribute make a difference?

Discrimination and judgment go both ways, as each side perceives ill treatment through a lack of understanding, respect, and willingness to be open-minded and equal in the interactions between the two sides.

- Who do you judge?
- How do you judge that which you don't quite understand?
- What prejudices have you formed through the effects of unresolved trauma around you or in you?

It is time to be completely honest within ourselves, as righteousness breeds ignorance and intolerance toward those who hold different opinions, perceptions, and ways of being from ourselves.

With whom am I in a power struggle?

My body says *everyone*, so I inquire, and it comes up that I am in a power struggle with the trauma of being mothered as incomplete.

I put everyone in the helpless-being-in-love-with-me category, as I am helpless in mothering a paradigm of existing as a focus of superiority.

My husband refutes that I am helpless. He points out other people who are helpless, as their lives and health have deteriorated considerably.

I say, "Just because I'm not strung out on drugs does not mean I'm not struggling with the same effects that make them helpless."

I depend on my husband to take care of me. I cannot easily belong. I hide in my house. I am not noticed when I post on social media. I am not acknowledged in the wisdom that I voice. My energy leaks out when I put effort into living. The experiences of childhood will not allow me to attach to beneficial support and healing that I do, as there is a lack of trust and safety in knowing positivity. And no matter what I do, the energy does not open up for me to experience relief of those effects so that I can gain the satisfaction of knowing that I have done a great job and get rewarded for my efforts. I will not push forward any longer. I need to keep trekking ahead in my inquiry to free myself.

Help, in the *Merriam-Webster Dictionary*, has three meanings that jump out:

1. Supply what is needed
2. Refrain from or prevent
3. One who serves another

I am outside, trying to talk through what is on my mind with my husband, while he hangs out the clothes to dry.

I ask him, "Do you know of anyone who feels *all together?*"

He says, "I believe that we are all working on something—or at least should be working on something—by being accountable to ourselves."

I believe there are more helpless people than there are people who feel whole or complete as they are.

Helpless people act out pain, which can be silent, dismissive, unacknowledged, unrecognizable, denied, or blatant.

I notice that some of us seem to get worse over time, instead of better. Why is that?

We get worse because of a mind-set that is an imprint of futility.

I have been imprinted with a way of being that is "personal existing branded as an ideation of misfit."

Attachment to the mind means deprivation of love.

Attachment to the spirit means self-sacrifice.

Women are sincere, as we all show up to serve. When I show up, it's not just about wondering what I can get from them. Some women trigger me, as they do not show up in integrity. But what exactly is integrity?

Integrity is being honest and consistent in character, which looks like the following:

> Reflecting and taking responsibility of your own stuff
> Working to see both sides of an issue, as both stories matter
> Not perceiving but knowing others as equal to you in importance
> Being welcoming and accepting of differences
> Identifying the power struggles (what triggers you) and working on them; being accountable and possibly asking for forgiveness
> Not attacking or suing people over perceived injustices toward self
> Performing service, which represents certainty of one's being whole but accepting support

Through personal experience and observation, I find that a lot of people who are in health, social services, or leadership roles do not progress in integrity. They try to fill an open hole within through acts of servitude, and they drain themselves of positive energy by giving too much of themselves by staying busy, popular, superior, and validated as wise or loved.

I have not accepted that I act out in integrity; I am indifferent to it because it was blamed for the undoing of family. I notice that when I am in integrity, I feel persecuted by valuing myself.

Service has represented certainty that I am incomplete, which traumatizes me when I make a difference, as being avoided doesn't allow my mind to see and experience that it is actually Athena that can create change. Having no perceived encouragement of conversion (seeing change in myself), I disengage from the satisfaction of knowing that it is actually me who asserts positive modeling and personal change. And this is because I have confused servitude with service. From me, service naturally comes from a whole heart of integrity, but servitude taught me that I can only serve someone by shutting me down so that the insecure can flourish.

This sends me to another layer to look at.

I was online, searching "personal branding," and thought I would reacquaint myself with how I picked the name "intuitive rebel" for myself. The definition of a *rebel* is someone who fights authority. I will admit that when I was younger, I did rebel against authority, as I didn't think authority was fair, and I certainly didn't think they had my interest at heart. Today, however, I just want the right to act as me. I have done personality tests, and one that said people will display one of four distinct and innate tendencies—oblige, question, rebel, and uphold—which has a distinct impact on how they become motivated to accomplish tasks and goals. When I googled "rebel," I found, "Rebels resist all expectations, outer and inner. They do what they want to do in their way and when they want to do it, acting from a source of freedom, choice, and self-expression. When someone else tries to get a rebel to do something, they resist. Identity is so important to the rebel."

I don't believe that anyone has a natural tendency to oblige, over-question, rebel, or partake in productivity perfection. We are all meant to act from a source of freedom, choice, and self-expression, in a way that uplifts our personal choices of living. When we are constricted or shut down from allowing that to happen, we then cope by instilling new ways to go about living our lives—usually in ways that we believe will have us fit in, belong, or make the grade.

More shadow work has come up for me.

The *shadow* represents the lie through which I see and express myself. I am still unclear as to what the lie is.

And my mid-back is hurting again. I had gone to get a massage from a woman who worked with animals, as one of her clients told me that she pinpoints the pain and releases it.

She put a machine on my back that vibrated. As it moved the energy within, I started to cough and then cough more deeply; then it sounded like a bark. *Was I a heavy smoker?* "No; I don't smoke," I replied. *Had I been in a fire?* No. *Had I ever been trapped in smoke?* No.

She couldn't explain this coughing and said she had never seen such intensity with a cough.

What I learned is that the body holds trauma, and this is what has kept me going as the mid-back (heart chakra) radiated pain at certain times.

When does it radiate and why? What is the meaning?

Closer to the end of the evening, a friend with whom I'd recently become reacquainted texted me to tell me of her nightmare. I tried checking in, through muscle testing, but the energy resisted.

Then she texted: "Athena! I think my nightmares mean you should be taking your meds." She worries about me. "It's a reverse sign. A way for me to connect then remind you."

Then I checked, using Wise Core Technique, and "proving we exist in a controlled world" came up.

I knew this was significant, but I needed to go to bed.

In the morning, intuition told me to think bigger—like, universe-instead-of-world bigger. Like, spiritually bigger over little-mind consciousness, which is where I am stuck.

This gets me thinking that most of us live by a lie.

The Universal Lie

We guide our way by the exposure to our tribe's way, without knowledge of how that way negatively impacts influencing our personal expression outward. We live through a truth that was never ours to own in the first place. This has us constantly striving to survive, rather than empowering self-expression toward thriving.

Is Depression a Chemical Imbalance?

My body brings up *no*.

Depression is self-regulating non-existent, as someone else's energy is internalized as one's own.

Depression is a result of essence being shut down from living.

Judgment

There is judgment when someone cannot or will not see the truth of someone or self.

To be able to stand strong in our way takes a lot of resourceful tuning in to the internal relationship that we have to the lies; becoming certain that we are complete in nature and embodying the significance of the real self showing up in any small or big way it chooses to do, no matter the judgments from others.

Not so hard, right? Yeah, right. Each culture has its own way to express its traditions, habits, and heirlooms. I see the headlines on the popular magazines of a woman's struggle with media in her right to govern herself, mother her child, and nurture her marriage in her own way, apart from what is expected (the society she was in expected her to be stoic, bury her feelings, which made her feel lonely, and uptight).

22

11:11

I WENT TO THE LOCAL remembrance service for those who served in the wars. The three-shot salute had me jump in insecurity. "What the fuck!" came out of my mouth. I didn't realize how sensitive I was—some would call it being an empath—as I was masking it well. My husband asked me in what way I was sensitive, and I said loud noises, judgment like sarcasm and indifference, the needle at the dentist, senseless killings, the change of weather, insensitivity, existing, and babies crying all make me cringe inside and want to explode with judgment on the outside. But I am also extremely sensitive to people accomplishing great things. I get choked up when a story of an Olympic athlete is televised, with pride for their journey.

I've realized how the lies of life connects us to negativity as being the *way*.

We identify with being a lie (something other than our true selves) rather than acknowledging that it is negativity that underlies an internal sense of futility we hold at the lack of power we have with encompassing positivity as the way to relate with ourselves in relation to one another.

War is useless and always has been. Hear me out!

War has a role to play. It commits negativity as being the presence of life.

War, I believe, is taught as the gateway to manhood for a lot of young men. How many men have enlisted in the armed services because their fathers did before them? How many males enlist before they are nineteen years old? It's easier to mold them at that age. How many children are enslaved to war? How many believe that the ones who die are heroes for signing up and serving?

Manliness—the traditional qualities of being strong and brave—seems to be valued only when found on the field; if not on the field of war, then in the streets of violence against each other.

While most women who lose their lives to homicide are killed by their partners or families, men are mostly killed by each other.

War against each other happens for many reasons: greed, power, dominance, corruption, possession, dogma, proving a group of people exist and that their rights are diminished, and control over someone or something.

War is most often life being irritated by a power-monger. A power-monger is someone who wields power in a tyrannical, irresponsible, blind, skeptical way and without consent and that ends up violating one's right to regulate positivity as the truth of how to live independently together.

Look at the leaders in power who glorify negativity with their staunch judgmental and irresponsible dispositions toward others, and then look at all the support those leaders receive from their followers.

What should we do with them?

Do not care about them! Do not feed their need to control their environment.

Do not give attention to their misplaced certainty that they are loved and revered as important in their acting out of negativity, which is critical to the independent presence that exists in positivity.

As a whole, we are obedient to negativity, as we are numb to our own truths. We have lost track of what feels right for us and what we should be standing up for *in a responsible way*, as we have been led to believe that negativity is the way, over our own innate truth within.

The media showcases negativity as reality, not realizing it's feeding the lie, all for ratings and a bigger paycheck. We watch it all; we fool ourselves into believing that it's a reality to revere.

23

IMAGINE

IMAGINE IF WE ENABLE OURSELVES to systemically and completely examine our traumas before the scarring takes place. Resolved trauma would no longer have the power to cause pain and suffering as a commitment to its being a reality of presence for the people we impact as love.

I recognize the commitment to suffer in my families as asserting love. Society at large knows suffering.

There are governments that are basically totalitarian. A totalitarian government doesn't see you as a human being. You're just a statistic, a number. And a number doesn't have to be appeased. A number doesn't have feelings or opinions that need to be considered. It just increases or decreases. But people aren't binary. People have ranges. People have feelings and opinions. They like different things, at different times, under different conditions. Censorship shows up and narrows the range. If you can control what people know, you can control what they think. You can make them more like numbers because numbers are easier to control. And when the people have had enough, protesting gets destructible, and lives often fall apart.

Why has protesting gotten destructible in nature? The government that encompasses control over the protesters who are encouraging their rights to be valid makes it extremely difficult to commit to democracy.

Is there a way to communicate, other than to protest?

Yes, and it is called compromise through peaceful debating.

Why don't more people/tribes peacefully debate?

They believe that there is no point in encouraging a connection between individuality and the larger scale of judgment (disrespect), as peaceful knows it will be acknowledged as not important, as it doesn't/ shouldn't exist.

What is the fear underlying this dilemma?

Most people are fearful of peacefully debating, as they believe to do so would encourage the danger of being recognized as weak, unreliable, untrustworthy, or racist, and so on. In being a danger, they assert us as being the cause of their disrespect, as they aren't conscious of positivity being a peaceful presence that wants to reinforce humanity's spirit as loving.

From where did this originate?

We can scale the protesting down to the peaceful individual in a family who is committed to negativity, and the knowing will be the same.

If we learned as children that we are the cause of our caregivers' suffering, then we become adults who are unsure of how to fully show up and stand up for the rights of self and others being considered important.

Let's move back to the larger scale of protester against government, companies, and organizations—they are misled from knowing their rights, to having to accept the propaganda's power to persuade. Propaganda has always been defined as a calculated attack on the complexity of other people's minds. Put simply, it's about political brainwashing to get the other person or people to submit without consciously realizing they are submitting. But know that brainwashing isn't reserved just for the political stadium; it is often bred as a family structure.

How do we change this momentum?

Start small with friends and family. Commit to speaking up for the truth and standing your ground on what you need to have happen for yourself. If you aren't regarded respectfully, walk away. Try again another time, but say, "I need _____ to happen for me to want to work together on finding a compromise."

Pay attention to your inner knowing. It might be hard to know whether you can trust it, but if there is no hurt, malice, judgment or insecurity involved, then you could be tapping into goodness. Be aware if you are numbing your feelings, as that would shut down awareness of intuitive hits.

To change the outcome on a large scale, we need to each start independently within ourselves.

We need to stop paying attention to the power-mongers who simplify complex ideas to have us submit to their consistent repeating of brainwashing to numb us, as this keeps us trapped in victimhood. We need to have an in-depth, thoughtful analysis into the truth, and that takes removing ourselves from paying attention to the headlines, tweeting, interviews, false online advertising, and editorials from left- and right-slanted columnists.

We need to get back to knowing our innate power of positivity that can influence change on a larger scale.

We need to reclaim our individual truths.

My middle boy has been out of high school for two years. We do not want to see him coasting for another year; he doesn't want that either. We want him to get a full-time job or go back to school. I signed him up for an open house at a college and drove him there. The day was scheduled from 10:00 a.m. to 2:00 p.m., but by 11:30, he texted me to say that he was out, as it was a waste of time. I told him to hang loose and to see what the afternoon would bring.

Half an hour later, he walked in the door, freezing, with blisters on his feet. He'd walked home, which I appreciated, but he wasn't dressed for it, as I'd planned to pick him up. He told me everything that had bothered him while he was there. He didn't think that the younger ones were taking it seriously, and he thought it was poorly planned. I felt guilty for not having picked him up.

I took time alone to process it more. It seems to me that I do not assume the best of redirecting negativity. I assumed that my son was being weak, restricting keeping an open mind on new experiences. But what was really going on was that he was discerning for himself what felt right and what didn't and that he was ready to leave when he realized he was in negativity. When I saw him later at night, I apologized to him, explaining how I saw him as being weak and that I had responded with cynicism.

But then I had to add that we both had to realize that negativity exists and that it isn't right to just walk out and hide. We need to face it by being true to self. We can ignore or work around it but we shouldn't run to hide from it, as that shuts us down from taking in what the moment can be for us in it.

I experienced a lot of immaturity around me in college in my last program of study, but I put my mind and heart into my studies and group projects and got on the dean's list for highest achievement.

24

MY DAUGHTER'S VISIT

WHAT AN EVENTFUL WEEKEND I had with my daughter when she visited.

On Saturday morning, I sat with her at the table, talking to her and asking about her business ideas. My husband was sitting in the adjoining living room, listening in. At some point, I could tell my daughter was getting irritated with me, and, as usual, I was unsure why. My husband stepped in by being supportive. *Am I not being supportive?* He said something that ticked me off so I walked away.

I went to check in ...

Self-inquire: Not having had anyone stand up for my significance, I am helpless in assuming that I am love in the moment. I am helpless, as I have a lack of reference for Athena being okay being Athena, so I get my sense of self from social cues. Am I liked as being okay or am I not based on gestures, facial signals, tone of voice, body language, judgment, etc.?

The following morning, I took my daughter to a craft show, and on the way home, I told her, "I sense that you feel off with me when you share."

She agreed that she did and said, "I'm not sure if you are trying to dominate and tell me what to do, even though I believe you are coming from a caring place."

"I have realized that I am trying to get my needs filled by my children, and I'm consciously paying attention to how I approach talking with you," I said. "I am intuitive, and I hear more meaning underneath everything you say, so I am trying to discern what you really want and where you want to go."

She said, "So you are trying to gather everything together and come up with themes that I say."

"Exactly! I am on your side. I have had dreams of working with you, but I am letting them go so that I can focus on supporting you coming into your own purpose."

Later that day, I was wondering what more I needed to do to own myself.

I need to assert a portrayal that I recognize me as a positive in purpose. But I am already doing this. My purpose is to come into the truth of self, first and foremost, and then to inspire my loved ones by my journey, and then to support the larger community in owning their value.

In the evening, before I went out to meet with a friend, I talked once more to my daughter about intergenerational trauma that was handed down. She denied having issues with love, but the next day, when she shared with me a few texts between her and a young man, I gently showed her where she was being cynical in creating trust with him.

It is vulnerable to let the defenses down and to let people in on the pain, discomfort, and suffering. It is vulnerable to face me, as I have not had sufficient attention to teach me how to care for me, regulate my temperament, or see the bright side of life with me in it.

It is scary to perceive the truth when, all along, that which I have abided by has been merciless to my existing.

This has been layer upon layer of self-discovery due to my being numb and shut down from me.

I have been awakening the whole time, and I have been making small changes in how I relate to me and to others as the layers come to the surface and dissolve in meaning.

I went to bed feeling good about me. I woke up with a tingling right arm and sore mid-back. What is my heart giving off?

My heart is giving off a danger signal!

Being me is a catalyst for rejection.

What exactly is *self*?

Self is a concept, derived from my being split that restricts essence (true me) from visibility in the now (present tense) to avoid the danger of vulnerability.

No part of me knew how to process and manage the shutting down of my personal existence.

My husband recently said that I have complained of the attitudes of each of my children toward me. I reflect on the formative years with my children and realize that I couldn't form a trusting bond with them, as I shut down every time they needed me to console them. I would say, "Go see your dad," as I believed I didn't have what they needed within me.

In not perceiving me as love, I irritated bonding by not offering me as loving to my children or husband. I was jealous in the early years of my husband's taking the kids to hockey.

In the early years with my children, I was able to parent the way my dad did. I took them outside and participated in activities, like going to the park, riding bikes, skating, building forts, tobogganing, and swimming. But being able to sit down with them and play Barbie or cars had me depressed (shut down from emotionally connecting in creative security).

"Look at me! But don't take me seriously, as I am a progress of futility." This has been a motto passed down. We want to shine and be seen as important, but when the collective energy restricts that way of being, then one can only feel hopeless in despair of its not happening. We do keep trying, but we see no progress.

I am trying to control me in how I show up, but when existence has been deficient in governing confidence in positivity as its way to be, then I am at a standstill as to how to proceed.

Actually, I have noticed that I am judging, being critical, or hostile with another friend and complete strangers. I am nit-picking at their insufficiencies.

What is underneath this?

Underneath sarcasm or criticism is personal judgment because of a lack of recognizing the self as important.

But I was satisfied with myself that I wasn't beating me up in recognizing this judgment. I noticed and, in that, was willing to make a change.

25

PERSONAL ACCOUNTABILITY AND FREE WILL

I WAS SHOCKED LAST WINTER when I walked down a busy sidewalk, and there was garbage lined along the edge. At the same time, I heard sirens, and I watched as cars pushed through the light, ignoring the emergency vehicles trying to get through. I created a video, sharing that I believed that when people feel a positive regard for their own value and self-importance, they then project the same respect for their environment and the people and animals residing in it. When we are trying to prove that we are important and that our needs come first, we jeopardize the good will that positivity is trying to enforce; often, leaves us taking for granted the good works and people in our lives.

I have been to a variety of counselors. My husband and I have both found that the majority of counselors do not have the skills to support people in taking personal accountability for their trauma drama. They keep us talking out the trauma but don't talk about how to successfully manage and move on from it.

Personal accountability is the belief that you are fully responsible for your own actions and consequences. It is a choice, a mind-set, and an expression of integrity.

I believe that it needs to start when we are young.

I have teacher friends who are frustrated with teaching boys who disregard them and talk down to authority. It's surprising when some girls send their teacher notes, thanking them for their efforts and apologizing for the boys' behaviors. Why do the girls apologize for the boys? I believe that we need to stand up to the attitudes and actions of bullies but not take responsibility for them by apologizing for their rudeness. We are not responsible for other people! They are responsible for themselves—or they should be. The boys should be held accountable for their own actions, and so should the girls. We each have to realize that we only have control over ourselves but that sometimes, that is restricted by the energy of family's love being restricted in valuing one another. The boys and girls who have a disregard for life and others come from a paradigm that stifles self-respect. Where does the paradigm come from?

Positivity of love builds us up. Negativity of judgment and control keeps us down.

I was lying in bed with my husband, talking with him, and he asked me what a self-concept was.

I answered, "It's only a concept! It's a perception that became real without any truth to back it. My pains are phantom impressions of hatred that surround me as life."

It is all false evidence appearing real, which represents as fear.

F—false
E—evidence
A—appearing
R—real

Free Will

As a collective, we see that the meaning of what free will entails is askew. We believe that we each should have free rein in how we live and make decisions, but we fail to recognize that a lot of people don't have an inner guideline of moral accountability to lead the way positively. What are the structures set in place that constrict freely choosing?

There are too many leaders in positions of great power who lack true free will, which results in the taking down of civil rights for democracy and capitalism. In situations like this, peaceful debate no longer works for finding common ground. This is when you need to shut down any damage from progressing by disengaging from those who constrict personal accountability. If they keep instigating trouble, keep shutting down. If they attack you, control engaging in gaining retribution, as that feeds proving their value in their negative behavior of constricting. (Think of Jesus's influence.)

Honest or the Truth?

Whenever I inquire, I ask if it is *honest* and if it is the *truth*, and I usually get opposing answers.

There is the story of me that I believe is the truth, but when I gather more information together, I realize that the truth has been hidden, manipulated, or misled or has been taken away from me; I rely on someone else's reality to be the truth, which is usually based on a lie.

If we look at dissention, hostility, or war, each side believes it is the honest one, but when you gather the sides together and talk out the differences, someone will uncover more information that makes up the truth, as the truth wants to be free from the lie.

Honesty and truthfulness are not the same thing. Being honest means not telling lies. Being truthful means actively making known the full truth of a matter (making the facts concrete), but if they unknowingly say something that isn't true, they are being honest (in the lie).

26

EMPATHY'S PARADOX

PERSONAL EMPATHY IS BLOCKED BY blindness from having no right to exist. When I try to share my experience, and someone speaks over me or steps in with judgment, I get heavy and feel deflated and defeated. Downplaying what I am sharing irritates personal empathy from being more than invisible, as it undermines my living and embracing my own reality.

Personal empathy is:

- understanding ourselves,
- knowing our feelings by being in touch with the inner vibrations of self,
- connecting with encouragement,
- letting go of owning or being responsible for the negativity,
- being kind to self, and
- forgiving self for losing sight of personal values.

I realize that not having a sense of self couldn't attach to concrete truths of self, so they flew away in the wind.

I am getting in touch with my emotional landscape but not so much to the inner world of energy, as I am blocked from connecting to encouraging my way as being a positive portrayal of self. When I get clear on something, I can feel the vibration go from my waist on up. I want to yell, "I get it! This is me, and I like me!" but I stifle it inside, as I can't show it as a portrayal of me.

I need to realize that I do show up. My friend said that when she met me, she liked me as the strong woman that I am, as I spoke up for myself in confidence. But I don't perceive that about myself. I intellectualize what is going on but don't embrace it with my heart.

It is time for me to acknowledge myself as a woman of inherent goodness who attracts positivity toward her energy, which is genuine of being welcoming to all.

Empathy

Empathy entails a deep engagement with a person's experience without judgment or interpretation. How many of us truly sit and listen without giving advice, trying to fix something, or judging it in some way? Can we fully listen and mirror the essence of what was said without wondering when we can put in our own two cents? I know my own empathy is constricted in its willingness to be sincere, but I am realizing this and am open to the energy changing through the light of love guiding me in truth.

I have seen "2:22" a few times, and I thought it meant to move forward into a new beginning, but I realize that it's an energy that is tricking me, to move me away from getting to the core of suffering.

27

PERSONAL EXISTENCE

SOME CHILDREN ARE BORN AS pure love.

➤ Some children are born, shut down from existing as a boundary of "separate."
➤ Some are constricted in narcissism as they become insecure in narcissism's having them prove that they abide by the narcissist's intentions.
➤ Addicts are born assured that they are incomplete.
➤ Those with self-injury are certain that they lack identities.
➤ Those who have had a sex change are certain of being inappropriate in their expression of identifying as significant as they are.

Someone told me that he is aware of transgenders (men to women) winning the fight to be in the Olympics as their chosen gender and that they blow their competitors out of the water. What? I'm not a specialist in this field, but by employing common sense, I see that a gender role from male to female does not change the fact that these males have had years of physically growing strength and size in their muscles. The cells don't forget the imprinting, and muscles don't forget the conditioning, and to pretend that all this doesn't matter is simply negativity blocking what is just for its own personal power, to gain satisfaction of being the best.

Is it right to put a woman's muscle up against a man's muscle? Again, the one to judge this as being okay is probably being pressured to uphold negativity as the way for fear of receiving "danger" (a backlash of persecution). A panel of judges needs to step up together to challenge the validity of what is being pressured to take precedence. Negativity can always be overruled, meaning that if you swayed on its side, you can always change course to get back to the side of honor ruling.

But then to flip the coin, what can be done with those who change sex and have the right to still exist, dream, and achieve? What would be the alternative? That would take healthy brainstorming and debating.

Flip the coin again. Why is there the changing of gender? It is becoming normalized when this practice is not meant to be for most candidates. This validating judgment of self as appropriate undermines any commitment to bring balance to making "less than" less permanent.

I AM THE HERO

"NEEDING TO BE THE HERO" keeps coming up for me now.

There is no Athena, only a boundary of hero. I am noticed as the caregiver who is the hero. Within my childhood roles, there was no recognition of *me* existing. I can only get noticed as the boundary of hero, as that is all that got developed as a reality of truth. With no personal intention, I am blind to self-existing as itself and not through someone else's energy of suffering and rejection.

To *intend* is to (1) have a course of action as one's purpose; (2) design or be destined for a particular reason.

My body is blocked from bringing up the core of this, but something wants to come up.

Existing is all mental. Essence being in presence is all instinctual.

I want to share an experience I had when I picked up my prescription at the drugstore. There was a man trying to get free drinks because they were advertised wrong.

The Scanning Code of Practice states "If the scanned price of a product at checkout is higher than the price that is displayed or advertised, the item becomes free of charge if the correct price is $10 or less."

He called the manager over, and she tried to tell him that this wasn't in effect for some reason. Then he threw the drinks down and yelled at her that she didn't know her own company's practice. After a debate, she said, "Take it for free."

He then yelled out at the people in the long line, "Make sure you get the right bar code scanned."

I looked at him and said, "Please keep your negativity to yourself, as this is only your issue."

"I am being positive," he said, "encouraging others to pay attention."
I said, "No, you aren't. It's negativity." And I walked out the door.

He seemed to think that warning everyone was positivity, but it was a condescending attitude, arising from the frustration of not getting his own way, whether or not he was correct in his account of the practice.

People are so unaware of what negativity looks like and how they interact with it themselves.

29

WE, AS HUMANITY, NEED TO TRANSCEND

WE NEED TO TAKE RESPONSIBILITY for our part in keeping the negativity alive.

We need to be accountable to ourselves, as no one can do it for us. We need to wake up to the truth, and the truth is that we are all love in any given moment, and it is up to us to believe in our sincerity to restore superiority to being love.

Misplaced Blame

When the mind doesn't want to face a particular instance, memory, experience, norm, or attitude, it will close off from the distress of it and project out its anxiousness, despair, or insecurity. In projecting helplessness, something heavy, negative, and discouraging lands on a receiver to hold and to become in tune with as his or her own. It is too much for the owner to bear, but for the receiver, essence is committed to invisibility, as this projection, becoming the main focus, robs the receiver of the positivity of self committing to his or her own truth.

Truth be told, misplaced blame lands only on the receiver if he or she is committed to encouraging negativity as being the way of love.

Not long ago, I wanted to punch my husband for pointing out something he wanted me to consider. My mind didn't want to consider it, but the truth of me did. I sat with it for a few minutes and then thanked him.

He helped me recognize that he wasn't judging me negatively or positively; he was only giving me another perspective to consider, which I felt I never had been given before.

Intensity

You can't help but feel just a little bit of jealousy. If you perceive that someone has something that you don't have and you feel "less than," then you are jealous. You are also helpless in recognizing that you are not lacking anything that makes you whole.

Jealousy is jealousy. Helplessness is helplessness. Own it. Then you can work on it.

Intensity is the feeling or energy that accompanies the emotion that sits in your belly and guides you into responding to the emotion. Jealousy hits; do you ignore it or dissociate from it (no intensity), judge it as bad (low intensity), yell in anger or make mean comments on social media (medium intensity), or pick a fight or pull a gun (high intensity)?

My way has been to dissociate from it; that is why my body revolts in pain. I hide out in my house, and I judge a presence as being negative in existence. Interconnecting essence with the distress of misplaced blame, I have committed my purpose to encourage powerlessness in my competence to love, as I validate their victimhood, more in need of existence than I am in living my own existence.

I have noticed that I look at my husband in a loving way. I can tell he appreciates this effort.

I have let go of placing blame on my parents, as they inherited this way from their parents, and my children have inherited this way from my husband and me (like attracts like). Blame doesn't help us realize how our competence in negativity regulates our loyalty in resisting living. Showing compassion creates a state of safety in being appropriate in the consciousness of negativity.

And my body tightens up even more. My husband says it sounds like I am getting sick, that I sound like I have a frog in my throat.

My chiropractor was surprised at the decline in structure since I last saw him a couple of years ago. I have a rib permanently out of alignment, and each side of my pelvis is opposite from the other. My neck's constriction in movement has inflamed the nerves, and my leg muscles are as tight as a baseball. I am in constant pain, and it gets worse when superiority is a prominent focus to me.

What Is Happening?

My nervous system goes into survival mode (the sympathetic nervous system) when I put effort into superiority. It has difficulty reverting back into its relaxed mode (the parasympathetic nervous system) when the damaged mind resists assuming the best of living, interconnecting essence with visibility. The nervous system stays in survival mode (high blood pressure) when the anxious mind detaches from internalizing a belief of personal power. Physical symptoms are a reminder of constant distress between the mind's being anxious of sincerity and the mind's pushing back against superiority functioning.

Why do I not take pills for my pain? Because of a certainty that it will make me helpless in expressing appropriateness.

Fuck. I am still stuck in denying love. My left ear into my throat and head are inflamed, and I have noticed that the veil between husband and me is still there.

Two parts come up on this:

1. This is more than the pain of a cheating boyfriend. This is an injury of a fundamental displacement of me in lovestruck. I was loving and being loved, and it was all taken from me.
2. I was deprived of primal mode's tenderness. Tenderness? How does this fit in?

My husband comes up behind me and wraps his arms around me, pulling my shoulders back, opening up my heart space. Emotion rises, and I start to cry.

What is love?

I believe I love and show love to my family, but these expressions are empty (they can't be fully experienced; anxiety is attached) because I don't have a capacity for knowing a portrayal of tenderness, so I don't know when or if it is safe for me to be secure in being me.

How will my self-portrayal be taken? I expect it to be attacked or judged as insufficient, so I've learned to shut down from expressing me in an appropriately free kind of way. Again, there is anxiety attached to my self-expression.

I need to get to the core of this anxiety.

Being damaged, I function in a mentality of inferiority.

Life does not happen to us; it happens for us. But we have our guards up and make excuses while we keep trekking along.

We all have compensatory behavior that constricts superiority. Most of us also deprive loving attention toward restoring living. Existing has become empowered as sovereign over assuming self-importance. Moving away from following through on healing only intensifies anxious existing.

We do this from a state of not knowing. We do not know where, when, or how the damage started, and so we are not conscious of these passed-down adverse effects, which influence us to distress our everyday efforts to subjectively nurture our power to live as a paradigm of essence, existing in the living of superiority.

What is the adverse effect that keeps me trapped?

The effect is a concept of perceiving me fundamentally incompetent.

Finally, it hit me. Incompetence keeps coming up, and I haven't known how to go about getting clear on the meaning—until now!

I was getting ready to go on a date with my husband and the thought popped up. I've come from a lineage of women who portray incompetence in taking care of themselves, being true to themselves, and in loving and being loved. And I follow in their footsteps, as though I identify with being the same way But in the last couple of days, friends have shared what they like and admire about me; there are so many positive attributes that I've realized that we women are conditioned to depress. And it shows that I have a marriage that others would love to emulate. I am not incompetent!

I was opening emails when one caught my undivided attention, as something seemed identical to something that someone wrote to me on Facebook.

The question I asked myself was, "What did I do to warrant such positive validation from these people?"

Email: "Athena, it's amazing that you are showing such bravery. Truly remarkable. The world needs more authors like you."

Facebook: "Athena. Thank you; you are such a beautiful soul! In the frequency of love and compassion, my heart is glowing knowing there are humans like you walking this planet."

Text: "This is why I love you Athena. I agree with everything you said. I love your honesty and that's what makes me confident to question what you say."

I didn't say or do anything out of the ordinary. To one, I asked a question, and to the others, I gave feedback that was asked of me, and it was neutral in meaning.

Is it about transparency? Yes. Do I wear masks? No, but I perceive myself as a mask—a mask of helplessness with being certain that I matter in my expression of self.

Self-inquire: My lower back always pings with pain when I recognize some truth about me. It's my nervous system emotionally flooding helpless when I connect to my truth. Certainty that life had no way of supporting me keeps the nervous system blocking my life making a difference for me. The instinct to survive controls how I associate with wellbeing for myself.

🦋 🦋 🦋

Something dawns on me. I have sent my oldest son an email to warn him of his dad's manipulation and to set strict boundaries so he doesn't find his life falling apart, like his dad's is. But my son only skimmed over it; he was not ready to look at his dad in a different light. And I got agitated with my son's being blind to how he is treated.

But I have made my son the victim when I shut me down from validating me as competent in raising him in positivity when he was younger. I didn't stand up to his dad's manipulation when my son was old enough to move in with his dad, so why now, when the roots are deep? I was used to negativity manipulating my blindness to the truth of their vulnerability to positivity, which had me automatically shut down a relationship, with regulating positivity as my way of what truth should be—I didn't know then what I know now. I didn't know that I felt helpless in manipulation. I don't feel helpless in it any longer, but I do feel helpless in being "Mom" for my son.

Weep all the sadness of disconnection and regret out, Athena.

Memory

My daughter brought something up to me, and I replied that I was curious how she got that idea. She said we had talked about it, and that's why she was bringing it up. I have noticed over the last few years that my memory is almost nonexistent. I used to say that my youngest boy had sucked all my memory for names and songs with his birth, but this is different.

Inquire: instilling a memory intentionally denied a commitment of positivity, encouraging me to assume the best of living, which left me with a paradigm of *pained objectivity*. So I am guessing that remembering names and faces and songs and artists was objective; thus, it was something my mind associated with. But where is Athena in this? She is nowhere to be found.

What is my mind then?

My mind is an ideation of anxiousness in attaching to existence.

30

PRESENCE WITH SELF

MY HUSBAND AND I WATCHED two movies, back to back, at home and decided to play some cards in between as a break. I said that the virus is keeping everyone from living, as we are stuck at home, existing. He said, "That's the issue: people don't realize that you live in the moment, not doing big things but just being yourself with where you are."

I tried to play cards, but I got emotional and felt anxiety rise up. I have been working toward traveling, making a big impact, moving away, thinking that is what living is about. But I was anxious in the presence of my loved ones, perceiving that I am not good enough or that I don't have what it takes to belong.

What exactly is still lingering in my chest? I went to lie down with my husband, as that is where insecurities come out and discussed on a relational level. My heart knows love; that's why I married my husband and brought three children into this world with him. But the mind, recognizing love as a validation of judgment, interconnects the heart with being committed to scarcity (never experiencing the wholeness of love, as the wall is up).

My husband does not judge me in the way that most others do. He has made me realize that children are not "supposed" to love us parents (they judge us all the time!), whereas a partnership between adults should be equal and supportive. Yes! My second counselor told me that it wasn't right for Mom to expect me to be the adult when it was her place to be one. I didn't absorb the implications of her statement until that moment.

Children are not meant to fill our emotional tanks. It is not their job to make our lives easier or to treat us a certain way so that we feel loved, appreciated, and valuable. It's not right for us to expect our children to take responsibility for our welfare, especially if we don't do it for ourselves.

I was trying to figure out why my ex—my oldest son's father—was irritating me so much. It's because he uses his son for his own gratification, but our son does not see his dad's influence of manipulation, as he has been tricked to view Dad as the man—the one to tell him how to do things, the one who knows all. I have referred to him as a Disney dad because he only wants his son around to have fun with and to boost his own emotional tank when he feels less of himself. My mom is the same way, and I didn't know it until I started this healing process. Their way is sneaky and slippery. But I won't disregard the positives between my son and his dad. My son has learned a lot of business skills from his dad and has done well for himself in business. He has also experienced a lot, which has him open-minded to new opportunities. But I can see the effects of his dad's influence with other people; my son allows other people to use him and take him for granted.

I have an equal partnership with my husband, but I have been anxious about investing my heart with him because of a certain group of people. With certain people (Mom, my sons, and a few clients), when fixing my attention on bonding with them, I am influenced to shut down sincerity when they consistently disengage from me, when I assume the best of my efforts in bonding. Why? Because they perceive my efforts, expressions, or portrayals as judgment on them, with me assuming the worst of their existence, all due to the shadow of the adverse effects of childhood.

What does the shadow represent? The shadow is an *alternative view*. Where there is only judgment, respective governing of regarding the other side is shut down from being considered.

And where there is only judgment, having attuned to it as a child, concept hasn't allowed self to give in to real love.

What is the outcome of this? I become numb, bringing me into awareness through bonding for fear of "adverse burdening of being," which was to shut me down from existing.

I distract myself from my husband's love because I don't believe the love of my husband exists because of the shutting down of primal attachment and the imprinting of self-importance on the inside.

My husband said that he doesn't say he is giving a different perspective when our boys get into sarcastic and sometimes mean ways (passive-aggressive) because he thinks it is common sense to us. I said it isn't common sense to us—or to me, who, only experiencing judgment, has a hard time acknowledging that it is actually positivity coming from my husband or positivity coming from me. I perceive that something must be wrong with me from the projection of passiveness from my husband and aggressiveness from the boys.

What a simple concept—my perspective and your perspective are equal, even if opposite in energy (positive and negative). We have to realize, though, that each energy embeds differently in existence through the attention from God.

Negativity enforces submission, while positivity empowers self to interconnect with love.

But when this concept isn't introduced and all that is accepted is negativity, then the mind assumes that any expression of self is an aggressive stance against the way of the majority.

Introvert and Extrovert

People often are confused on what constitutes introvert and extrovert characteristics.

Shutting down and shutting you out from the world is not because of introverted tendencies. It's because you are depressed. Being nervous about speaking up, feeling drained at a party and hanging out in the corners, and being shy are considered normal tendencies for an introvert, but it's not done naturally. It's because you are anxious about allowing your real self to manage respective, (separate/individual) truthful living.

Intuitively, I perceive that it's how we process information and not how we interact with people. Then I realize that it is the mind that processes, and the mind is what controls the personality. So, Higher Knowing, is there such a thing as introversion and extroversion? Not to the higher self; it is the lower self's paradigm of learned helplessness in perceiving the truth of self in the light that has labels for every expression of perceiving incompleteness. Lower self labels; the higher self empowers right judgment but not using it as a label for the person (example: narcissism tendencies (H.S) vs the narcissist as a personality (L.S.)).

I wasn't recognizing that I perceived the higher self as a separate entity from me. And, I am not in-tune with the play out of subjectivity's energy being introverted or extroverted in its expression as subjectivity, as a personal association of mine, has been shut-down from being innocently displayed.

31

THE MIND

I WAS READING EMAILS FROM work and a wellness one caught my eye. It read, "Keeping an Open Mind in Balance During this COVID Crisis." In yoga, there are three yogic mind centers: positive mind, negative mind, and neutral mind. I did not know about a neutral mind but it makes sense that if there is another perspective than the judgmental way I have known, then there is a mind other than the negative one I have known. I have thought that it was the positive one, as there is negative and positive energy. Is there also neutral energy? Yes. For my simple knowledge base and the difficulty of healing my own self, this was big news to me!

Let's get clear on the states of mind:

The negative mind: reactive; commits to power struggles, judgment, futility, and anxiousness that burdens superiority by shutting down its existence.

The positive mind: constructive in progressing autonomy; empowered to follow through with nurturing bringing self up and forward as well as powered by personal accountability, encompassed by sincerity of integrity. (You cannot have integrity without sincerity.) The positive mind internalizes superiority as a paradigm of existence that empowers nurturing a clear yes to living.

The neutral mind: (This took work to bring up!) It is not a mind to consider; it is a way of being. This state is a commitment of essence integrating a portrayal of truth with the clear yes to love of self. When I was little, I innately knew my importance, as well as everyone else's, and I loved with no mind attached to it. I existed as instinctual being. I knew how to live; no one had to teach me. If I would have interconnected with positivity, an imprint of truth would have empowered personal focus to attune importance with subjective living. But for me, the power of negativity took the reins and changed not only consciousness, as it was traumatized into zoning out, but instinctiveness, with its persistent judgment.

The paradigm is neutrality and positivity being committed to nonexistence, which shut down managing competence in internalizing self as complete.

In shutting down neutrality and positivity, the mind attuned to turning inward in suicidal, knowing it was dangerous to put expressions of complete out there.

I took a break to eat an apple streusel. My nose gets itchy when I eat certain sugars. But this morning, before I ate that sugar, my nose itched. What is the common denominator in the itch? It must be the focus on love, specifically self-love. But it isn't; it's more specific. It's a distressing of any commitment to positivity of self being visible in living.

I had a conversation over lunch with my husband, saying that I think he puts me on a pedestal and judges me at the same time. He said he does challenge me with other perspectives, and he does see my flaws and is willing to speak up when I am being less than myself. I see. Essence knows but my mind does not know love as an expression toward mothering complete, which overwhelms the mind, connecting to being lovable or loved.

I have noticed a theme of not caring.

From my clients to my sons, they don't care for their well-being or for themselves, as they do not seem to care about self. I know that I didn't care about me until my son was born, and then he opened my mind to another possibility. But being honest with myself, I still don't care for my well-being as I want to be. So what's this really trying to say?

The answer came to me from a spiritual counselor that I used at least ten years ago. I absolutely felt safe in his presence. I phoned my organization's company, which would set up counseling for me after a run-in with a client. One night, I was verbally assaulted and was being triggered. I called in for relief and went home. I could tell by my going home that it was considered a win by the client. I went home and worked on the trigger so that the following evening, I could show up with my intention of not taking it personally. As soon as I walked in, the verbal assault started, so I asked the day staff to stay for a few minutes and witness.

The client threatened to hurt me, kill me, and then burn me. I was not scared, so I stood there and tried to redirect, but I was shaking inside, as I took it personally on some level. Then the client suddenly broke out in tears and apologized to me, saying that they didn't know what had come over them. The client brought up old traumas of abandonment and then told me to hold their lighter, as self wasn't to be trusted with it.

The shift went well after that. But I was confused on how to follow through after breaking down the wall of distrust, as the client was still resistant to my asking them do something.

The counselor broke down what had happened:

The client didn't care about self and was going to do everything in its power to bring me down and have me prove the client was no good by walking away. But in my not abandoning, I didn't prove the client as no good. The client saw goodness in my willingness to be present and apologized for the outburst.

The vulnerable need to protect themselves, and if we make their behaviors about them, they will defend themselves. Fear is under venom. If people feel cornered, they will thrash out.

When we take it personally, they pick up on the energy of our being emotionally removed, and they feel abandoned when the support isn't there for them when we've made it about ourselves. When we face it head on, it shows care on all levels of presence, and they integrate with trusting expressions of love and care.

Getting individuals, who are indifferent to their own lives, to take direction in doing something that is asked of them (but for them) is an uphill battle. Do for them, hoping that you will influence the same behavior from them down the road. I know of a few men whose moms did everything for them when they were growing up, and when the males left home, they attended to their lives to get the same results that they'd received when Mom did it for them (ingrained outcomes).

I have learned that there is no motivation to do for self when there is no assurance of safety, security, importance, or value in doing so.

This is my perspective: for the ones that identify as assured in expressing competence in wanting more, we need to have them be involved in creating change in their lives but not by enabling by doing for them. We need to do it with them, by encouraging a belief in the importance of their being competent in their capacity to do for themselves. It might be an uphill battle to encourage self-sufficiency because of unresolved trauma that dictates competency, but keep at it, as the motivation is there to work with.

We need to be consistent in being present and not taking a negative attitude personally. When we take it personally, it's our trauma that needs attention that comes out to be noticed and cared for. In our trauma, the weakened will shut us out and keep them down in futility.

There is another point here: when kids don't get their relational needs met, they blame their parents (shifting from parents to authority) for their hardships. They can turn into adult children who still hold blame (mental diagnosis is sure to come from this), trying to get their parents to prove that their children matter to them, all with underlying hostility. There is a mix of need and blame that takes over the child's, then adult's mind.

For those whose motivation or willingness to commit to themselves is blocked from governing independence, we, as support, will either find it difficult or easy to be effective in connecting them to self-competence. Staff needs to portray competence in redirecting negativity. Those who are validated a clear yes to influencing homeostasis as positivity will be competent in getting the client to change direction, but those who are validated a clear no in influence will experience resistance by the client.

Personally, my power to influence certainty of being competent in rejecting negativity as the way is devoid of the existence of support to subjectively manage independence with positivity. With no support and no positivity, I have given up on trying to act as if I can express complete and influence positivity in demeanor.

The numbers 2:22 keep coming up around me; its meaning is that I need to recognize positivity as the essence of me being present.

Out of nowhere, this realization hit me. *I am not normal!* I have lived a life that most would only dream about. And then this sadness comes over me; actually, it's more like grief.

Self-Inquire: trauma of being rejected and abandoned is all vulnerable to the suffering of not being considered normal. Do I truly want to be considered normal? Yes. Why? Because it is appropriate to belonging. Children need to know that they are normal and that they belong to validate themselves an effect from the cause. Cause is appropriate parenting, and effect is belonging as an impression of love, commencing out of appropriate parenting.

My daughter wrote out an insight that validates me before I became conscious of this for myself. "Everything that I have done is an expression of trying to figure out who I am and where I belong."

Everything that I have done has been hands-on teaching to encourage people to see themselves as competent in stretching out of their limits. But instinctively, I've pulled back. I have had too many instances of either being judged for something that I have said or done or not having validation of being whole in self-expression, and I am not open for attack or rejection any longer.

What theme is going on right now?

A friend wanted to do a craft over the webcam, and I wanted to yell, "Fuck no!" I said I wanted to get gardening going, but someone brought up ideas of how to create one, and I wanted to yell, "Fuck no!" I don't want to make masks for this COVID-19 virus, even though I have the equipment to do it. I don't even want to think of having to wear a mask.

And then, after dinner, as I was doing the dishes, my husband asked me if I was saving the strawberries for a smoothie, and I replied, "It matters what youngest son wants."

And my husband asked, "But what does Athena want?" And I wanted to cry. Has it ever been right for me to put intentional effort into making me a priority? No. And then I saw this quote on social media, and I wanted to cry: "No matter how much self-isolation I do, I watch those in my community who ignore social distancing and mask recommendations and know that my odds of getting sick increase exponentially in direct response to the stupidity and inconsiderate behavior of others."

What is really going on with me now?

I am having a hard time recognizing me as positivity because of being personally considered a burden by living my life that feels right to me.

What is it about *personally* that I am not getting?

This grief of regret comes over me because even though I have worked hard on my efforts to support the truth of my children, I believe that I have already done the harm of reinforcing anxiety with their existence. This is *personally* taking responsibility for any weaknesses I perceive.

Personal represents internalizing existence as a paradigm of respective living (acknowledging and empowering the paradigm of self—love, positivity, sincerity, integrity) separate from the others.

I feel so congested.

I am sensitive to judgment and keenly aware of inappropriateness due to my ability to recognize a distinction between negativity and a portrayal of competence in positivity. But instinct of portraying this has been shut down to living competently in the present moment by the humiliating of me in positivity.

I have been painting my life with a belief that selfishness is wrong and that it injures belonging.

The clock reads 10:10. This means I have to shut down the existence of assuming the worst of my reality. What's my reality? I am anxious to attach to me as love because of shutting down respective empowerment of instinct.

I have wondered why I wanted a connection with Mom when she left.

It is clear to me now that I believed it was my selfishness of not getting along with her that created the suffering; that if I worked on getting along with her, the suffering would vanish. Because I believed that I was the problem, by pretending that everything was right with us, I perceived that the suffering vanished, even though it got worse.

My state of being has been proving that I am the primary cause of systemic breakdown (internally and externally) when I am selfish, expressing complete.

In that moment, I checked into the deeper *why*, but nothing concrete came up.

I got the phone call I'd been expecting, and halfway through, I told the speaker that I was deflated and didn't want to move forward with this matter at the moment. The phone call was my answer. I am in tune with smooth-talking, confident salespeople who dupe me into paying for services that I am unsure have good value.

We are all salespeople when we connect to each other to cause an agreement on what will be done and how it will get done through integrity. But most of us are definitive in validating manipulation competent in portraying integrity. We have accepted salespeople and leaders as efficient when they are competent in getting us to do what they want (mind control) in their way, but they make it look like it's what we want, need, deserve, or agreed to.

But isn't this persuasion? I want to get better at persuading people to accept my work, and I don't believe there is anything wrong with that.

The difference between manipulation and persuasion is that persuasion validates the positivity of committing neutrality to presence. Manipulation doesn't give consent for your voice to rise up; it is blind to the competence of one's discerning what is good and what is not for self. It will distress you as you try to redirect to gain clarity so that you connect to the competence of the manipulator who controls the outcome.

I need to realize that manipulation is so deceitful and sneaky in disguise of being beneficial. I am attracted to manipulators because of the competence of Mom committing me to exert her lies as the truth, while disarming me from knowing my truth. I need to stop them in their tracks, second-guess their intentions, and ask direct questions to get clear on what is being offered before I say yes, sign on, or trust the message of hope for something beneficial, when I do know what I need to move me forward in the light.

Let me ask you: how many times have you been lied to, cheated on, judged, taken for granted, used, or ignored, and how often have you turned the other cheek, believing that you do it all for love, to belong, be accepted, and be connected in your relationships? That is negativity taking over your reins, empowering transparency in integrity of connecting together.

You have given your power away to someone who only thinks of what you can do or offer to them in that moment. Let's face it: most of us have been there, done that, so we shouldn't be pushing people to the side because we're offended. We all deserve compassion and the chance to take accountability to make things just. But we also shouldn't let things continuously slide out of awareness, as that creates anxiousness in attaching to becoming more of the real you as you give your power over to the opposite side.

Most of us sit in futility of the truest self being free to live in the light, and instead of acknowledging it and speaking up for more, we escape personal accountability and zone out from subjective powering of sovereignty. The more I take of this journey into the truth, the more anger I feel at the injustice of being shut down from the importance of focusing on reinforcing proof that truth is superior too.

Personally, I am helpless, validating what will actually serve me versus what others are trying to sell me as being complete. The real issue is that I don't identify with truth as a mothering of the real me showing up. I know what is right, which makes me helpless in expressing complete.

Moving forward, I need to make a big decision that could change my course of action, and I notice that presence is petrified of how I recognize manipulation that tries to make me swoon into perceiving them as correct in their implications. What is under petrified? Recognizing manipulation implies danger of agency being disabled from committing to effective regulation of independence and free will because manipulation (a structure of shutting down agency) irritates appropriate power of determining independent freedom of choice.

In social science, *agency* is defined as "the capacity of individuals to act independently and to make their own free choices." By contrast, structure (e.g., being validated as negativity) is a factor of influence that determines or limits an agent and its decisions.

Complex trauma creates predictability of invisibility in the structure of *less than*, as it has the mature person shutting down superiority in anxiousness of attaching to existence. Attachment structure gets activated by constricting existence, when anxiousness numbs governing superiority. Anxiousness numbs when being acknowledged as established inferiority. Are we actually being acknowledged as inferior, or is our survival brain constantly activated for judgment, and we create it to prove it right? Mental energy is bound up in the shutting down of superiority, empowered by anxious, existing as a reality of superiority.

Personal power to act consciously and intentionally numbs authority from executing sovereignty over anxiousness attaching, as it has been shut down from engaging in love. A shutdown from love denies authority competence in portraying the truth of self, which impacts presence being distressed by the blocking of believing self is value.

To what do I give power to execute sovereignty over self-value? I give power to the appraisal of inferiority. I don't see me in the interaction of offering *more than*; I am in tune with the existence of negativity, to which I commit authority to blindly enable their competence in the power to define value. Self-value dissociates in the authority of "I'm superior (female) and denial of competence (male)."

After the exchange, something irked me (anxiety of having an opinion), and I questioned my ability to discern the authority of certainty of which I was under the influence. My husband walked in the room, and I asked him for a word that would encapsulate what I was expressing.

He said, "Actually, Athena, this is normal for a lot of women. Men do not see them as being equal, and that's what the feminist movement tries to change. Masculinity is superior to femininity in the eyes of 'women are only good in their designated social roles.'"

Yes! This has become normalized in societies all around the world, but it doesn't make it just, appropriate, or true. It impacts authority, dismissing self-competence, as what's the point in being more than judgment when judgment redirects attention away from powering up the presence of equality?

🦋 🦋 🦋

This weight of futility keeps pushing me down.

Note: there are a variety of "invisibilities" with which humans are violated upon conception and into developing a way of being.

I know I can keep going with the layers, but I need to know the main thread that attaches them. The main thread is: interconnecting presence with portraying truth as "self is suppressed from knowing truth is self when competent in visibility."

It's serendipitous, as this just came up in an interaction between my men and me. Oldest boy came down to eat breakfast, and he grabbed a bowl of sugared cereal.

My husband said to him, "At one point, you wanted to be a trainer. You should have started off with an apple."

My son didn't care about that statement.

I piped up and said, "I just talked about this with a girlfriend. She said she didn't allow her children to eat sugared cereal until the weekend. And that is where I am fucking up."

My husband didn't say anything.

And then the truth hit me, and I said, "I can't say that as the whole truth because this is a more recent phase. I used to control the sugar of their diet."

My husband agreed. What happened here was that I was competent in validating the way I do things as being recognized inferior by them, but I recognize my attempts at love as failure.

I patted myself on the back as I challenged my own perception of me as defective in some way.

Why do I cry when I think of my loved ones?

More specifically, I struggle with being honest with my oldest boy. I know I love him unconditionally, but I've noticed that he is influenced by his father, and my son thinks it's positive in regard for him. I see that his dad is making my son a "mini him." I congratulated him on an accomplishment that took my son about six years to complete, and I cried while I was texting.

I had a sense that he believed he had to choose between me and his dad, but this was far from the truth. I told him so, and he said, "Dad is trying to get me to make him a favorite, but I have a wife, so this has been a struggle, having Dad here for so long a visit."

Thank you for stating that, son, as it brings to awareness that your dad is a lot like my mom (my normal). My mom manipulated the males into taking sides, and they chose her over believing in me. It sounds like my son's father is trying to get him to take sides.

Conviction: males are weak in standing up for what is right and just.

Conviction: females encourage males to turn on what is right and just.

Conviction: I am not lovable enough to be considered a portrayal of significance, which makes me powerless in my competence with positivity.

Conviction: I am irrelevant. (I keep hearing stuff from my boys, such as that I don't know what I am talking about.)

I can intuitively tell there is more, but it is resisting coming up.

I can't sleep. I get up and look at the time: 4:44 a.m.

I look up the meaning: "Every decision I have made has been influenced by divine intervention."

But the free will to awaken this interconnection is in the shadow of judgment.

Self-Inquire: as an embryo, I was committed to judgment. In existence, it was futile to be competent in committing presence to positivity within the power struggle of the shadow of judgment. Committing presence to positivity validated my shame of being visible. I lack recognizing me when I am being competent in positivity because futility shuts visibility down from perceiving competence as a good attribute of self. I am normal, portraying me as shame in visibility, as "the whole." Being encouraged to interconnect the presence of me as being less than positive makes me faithful in downplaying competence in love, in recognition of love being me.

How depressing! No matter of what I become conscious or what changes I choose to make, nothing intentional becomes concrete in a conclusion of complete because of the need to mature a clear no to the consciousness of knowing truth as right and just to implement.

When I check in nowadays, there is another energy that influences the answer. I have to ask for "the truth of Athena only" to come up. I believe it's about the majority outweighing the minority of love.

The truth for Athena is that she is alone in existing in a paradigm of value (empowering superiority to align personal power with the self as whole.

But is she really alone? No. Athena can't recognize support and care of her way because of the follow-through of the majority for most of her life, shutting down awareness to value.

Even though I am doing this work to resurrect my way as important, I shut down following through with trusting soul tie to align with me assuming the best of my exiting. I am keeping myself alone, insecure and perceiving personal attacks, because of my experience of being all and nothing. I was all to blame and nothing special to have around.

I have experienced a lot of goodness in my life, and it didn't come because of my mind having willed it. My husband knows that I don't believe it was self that made the choice to be with him; it was "a knowing" that he would be good for me and that I would feel safe with him that brought us together. (I actually thought it was a force outside of me that brought us together, as essence wasn't part of my reality. I have since recognized that it was me who made the choice because it felt right to do.)

I knew I was pregnant with the last two boys the moment they were conceived. When we finally made the decision to sell our house, it was the knowing that it was time that brought the first interest to buy our house, and the first house we looked at, we bought. The process of selling and buying was smooth and profitable.

I need to ignore the headaches the mind creates in fear of being validated a misfit because I am strong in my awareness that I am competent in following through on my knowing what is right for me and what isn't.

Mind-sets are concepts that align superiority to assume the worst or the best of existence. To undo and disable these concepts, we have to dissolve the paradigms that numb aligning superiority with assuming the best of following through with restoring living.

What paradigm is trapping essence from being visibly attuned with the existence of an established sense of self?

I am insecure in restoring superiority, now that I have identified that it is lovestruck that gets "personal" shut down. It's implied that the whole of lovestruck will shut me down when I express my way, as that was my childhood reality. Today, I need to realize that the whole is more of a quarter that is anxious to attach to me, and it's all because they have their own norms from which to release blindness. To the other three-quarters who want to engage with me, I push them away in implied "suicidal" of abandoning me when I express the truth of me.

Essence, interconnecting to the life of truth, has access to everything that is more than the lower self of judgment and norms of negativity.

Have you noticed that it is higher self that provides the answers, in the knowing of the whole truth, apart from what the senses inform our perceptions and states of being?

Essence is committed to the positivity of being recognized as the source of healing, but it has dawned on me that personal is blind to what positivity is to this personal resurrection, as personal is blocked from identifying with positivity. Anything concerning me and my own reality being the way to live was never a consideration to the family into which I was born. Instinctively being positive from the get-go was shut down from the maternal notion that personal cannot exist.

Consciousness

The brain develops competence in interconnecting presence with positivity when conditions are favorable toward the positivity of the truth being visibly validated as complete.

There are two references of positivity here: one is a state of being and the other is a state of upbeat focus and attention. What exactly is positivity? It is competence in interconnecting presence with self-portraying an expression of wholeness. What exactly is competence? Competence is this interconnection that matures a mind concept that validates self as complete.

I am realizing that to give life meaning, one must know oneself as complete.

Unknowingly, I have made my life a quest to resurrect personal meaning (self-worth, importance, efficacy, sovereignty, value, personal existence). But I didn't know that expressing *complete* wasn't safeguarded from injury and that it's this injury that blocks me from being certain of having personal meaning.

For me, meaning represents "of or concerning one's private life, relationships, emotions and an expression of Complete rather than acting out helplessness in validations of acting as if you are complete."

Heal this injury; pour love, forgiveness, and grace all over this rift to repair it.

I thought this was done, but then anxiety did a somersault in me, so I know there is more.

How does self recognize my husband as positivity?
Self believes he commits to me as broken, needing empathy.

Influence of Romance Novels

My husband and I were talking in bed. He asked me, "What do you want?"

I said, "I want someone to travel with, have coffee on a balcony with, walk hand in hand with and kiss on the veranda."

"That sounds like a Harlequin romance that you're enforcing as the way to love," he said.

I hadn't made that connection! In my earlier life, I would read books that were intimately steamy in detail—the woman gave herself freely to the man who had confidence and charisma. Over the years, I moved to watching romance movies that started off with the woman having a wall up; the man would show that she could trust him, and they would fall in love. Sometimes I read novels with faith added in. But to what was faith added? Love? No, it was positivity. Isn't positivity love? Yes, but being validated judgment, self doesn't recognize positivity as love; only judgment is recognized.

At first, the steamy romance novels were an escape from judgment. But as I matured in life, romance novels evolved to encouraging positivity into existence. Today, I look to these books and movies as role models for how to be competent in maturing positivity as homeostasis of life.

Competence is committed to suffering by the mind that judges the existence of knowing love and making it visible as "broken": having been fractured or damaged and no longer realized as competent in positivity as love.

ATTACHMENTS

I AM ATTACHED TO A way of being. The way of being is "respective judgment." Everything about me (subjective, intrinsic, self-importance, existence, positivity, superiority) was judged wrong in some way and always in a different way. I enveloped this judgment as personal; judgment is me. So no matter where I find myself on the well-being trail, I will sabotage it so that I bring me back to the homeostasis of judgment.

I know some sort of deprivation needs to come up. I was sitting at the window again, talking to my angels, and emotion came up, with this revelation: "a part of me wanted to die; the part that was connected to suffering." Suffering was a structure created from positivity having no space, approval, encouragement, or right to exist—never mind growing and developing.

The numbers 11:11 show up: a message from angels to suggest aligning superiority with assuming the best of my power to resurrect the importance of believing that attaching to the inside will progress a contributing to structuring a bond with my reality mattering.

Oh, this is coming from my dreaming of leaving the house to the boys' care, buying a trailer, and traveling with my husband. But I ask myself if I am looking at doing this because I have had enough of not belonging, so I need to escape, or is that I am trying to find a place to fit in and belong, or is it that the spirit of me wants to do it for the fun of the adventure?

What is my truth?

My youngest boy's media teacher phoned to say that my son is not handing in homework. He said I can go to Google Classroom and see what he is assigned to do. After the call, I went to absently eat something as I thought about this. *Can I honestly get online and check? Why have I believed that I don't have the ability to be competent in figuring things out and supporting what needs to get done?*

I felt weak, as self-confidence in competence in doing what needs to be done to parent or marriage is low. Why? Because valuing me, my capabilities, and my contributions was nurtured to be incompetent in its ability to thrive, separately or as part of the family.

That's why I had felt low, with no sense of purpose—no sense of value; no purpose.

Undo, detach, disband, dismiss, disable this mind of low value that plays out as incompetent in my competence.

Life once again showed me that it supports me on my journey. From teachers phoning, to something happening at work, to a child approaching me or feeling abandoned of caring, life showed up to play out that which I needed to look at to help me grow into the person I am meant to be.

I have noticed that I hold my breath after I exhale. And then as I've worked on this, I've noticed that I squeeze my sphincter involuntary.

Self-inquire: I disengage to shut down acknowledging the denial of being pained.

One way I am pained is that I let people over-talk with me. I am blind to being used in them proving that they are appropriate in their expression while I down play being real and heartfelt (a state of being sympathetic). I am enticed by the head strong that are loyal to believing that they are submissive (so giving). I am the submissive one; their needs become my needs. I am a shrinking violet in the pattern of resistance that I know comes from them, the head strong.

33

MENTAL ABUSE

I ASKED MY HUSBAND WHICH emotion, other than grief and sadness, was weighing on me.

He said, "I have heard from people on podcasts that it is often a case of 'overwhelming crushing unworthiness.'"

Those words feel heavy to me.

Self-inquire: overwhelming, crushing denial to recognize me as I truly am makes me competent in barricading myself against love.

My husband brought up the subject again. He said that when we were children, it was normal for physical abuse to happen. The hand was used, as well as the wooden spoon (I had one broken on my behind) and the belt, plus soap in the mouth. Heck, even the priest and nuns that visited during school hours had a ruler they used to whip our outstretched hands. You could hit in public and nothing would be said about it.

I said, "Just because it might have been normal doesn't mean that it didn't damage someone's identity."

He replied, "Athena, I think we all suffer from adverse effects of some sort of physical abuse, but I think you are still trapped by mental abuse."

Why have I not identified it as mental abuse that suffocates my existence?

Self-inquire: maturing mental abuse as an experience of positivity had me develop actual positivity as a respective existence apart from love. This way has encouraged positivity to redirect interconnecting self with love, validating love as "competent in suffering in visibility."

Are positivity and love one and the same? Yes! Being committed to suffering denied me a validation of love, so positivity represented presence in portraying truth.

Once I realized that I had the power to pull my son aside to encourage him to show me Google Classroom, I sat next to him as he showed me page after page. I apologized for not being a bigger part of his learning experience. All went well. I was not aware of how I then shut down to the experience of love that happened; all I recognized was my body burning on the inside the next day.

My husband pointed out that the day after I have a loving session with him, I find something that irritates me about him.

Impact: in me being me, I shut down to committing to admitting that the truth of me is love. If I were to admit that the truth of me is love, I would have to admit that my entire childhood was a lie, making me deficient in life. In life, I lack an interconnection of presence with truth, which has made for an experience of suffering.

How did I have to be with the men in my life in my childhood? I had to be invisible so that I wouldn't get attention from them, as that would get me envied by Mom. But how was I to be invisible? Depress positivity from being in existence. I can recognize how this has played out for me. One of my college courses was mostly attended by males. The males liked me, but I didn't acknowledge that. I just noticed how a certain female got all the attention. I didn't allow myself to fully flow in the attention of interactions, as I was disconnected from having the essence of me shine.

The same happened in my relationships with men. I would start off strong in kissing them, but by month four, I would disengage from fully being there. I tuned out satisfaction, the more they got into me. With my marriage, the more he got into me, the more I disengaged. With my children, the more they developed and were able to form trusting engagement with bonding, the more I disengaged from showing up.

I am there but as concept (because the "real" me doesn't belong) because I block the energy of making a mark as positivity. Concept is what energy? It is the energy of scarcity. (I lack making a mark as positive in nature.)

Our daughter texted to say that the fire department told her and her roomies that they have to vacate their apartment ASAP. I texted back to give her options and to suggest that she call the tenants board. My husband texted her to say that he was sorry for them and that they must be upset about the situation. I told him that he was being empathetic, and he said that he is always empathetic. I haven't been open to really seeing that part of him until now.

I went to work, thinking about empathy. When I got there, I asked a staff member, who is a social worker, to help me out. She said she really appreciated knowing that I am one of a few who is working on her stuff on her own. Then she said it is "emotional empathy" that I'm struggling with because of a fear of being vulnerable.

That is true. I can intellectualize care and support but lack emotionally connecting because of the vulnerability of persecution in building bonds with loved ones. I find it hard to give of my heart, to put the whole me into soul-to-soul interactions. I don't invest the sensitive parts of me. And I know my spine, representing life, holds on to the impact of the persecution.

I am strong in *cognitive empathy*, which is the ability to understand how a person feels and what that person might be thinking. *Emotional empathy* (also known as affective empathy), the ability to share the feelings of another person, is shut down as the traumatized mind of being validates a mistake. The shutdown of emotional empathy injures connecting to those I dearly love because it makes it certain that bonding is empty of compassionate safeguarding of *complete*. Having no one protect me against Mom's mistrust and suspicions so that the males could feel safe in bonding with me has blocked me from recognizing the need my loved ones have for a soul-to-soul engagement with me. My soul aches for the whole of me to attach with another soul that needs me, wants me, and loves me.

My emotions get triggered by the experience of fulfilling or terminating a demonstrating of love as truth, which translates to love as self.

34

CONTROL

Trying to uncover and understand the complexities of
being human are hurting my mind!

CONTROL IS BEHIND MOST EVERYTHING in life, past and present.
Control is not associated with the real self of love, truth, and neutrality.
Control is a mechanism of the mind that threatens certainty of a validation
of complete by beloved (self is created perfect/complete by source).

I have anxiety with validating me as neutral in my competence in love.
(Most of us reside in this energy.) I am anxious because neutrality (essence
of me), never having been brought to light by the shutdown of love, isn't
recognized by the humanness (positivity, negativity, body, mind, heart,
validation of incomplete) of me when soul does commit to my competence
being love.

Soul is a piece of God, established beyond doubt complete, validated
by Beloved.

This piece of God interjoins with the embryo's mind of humanness.
But if the mind of humanness is injured by effects of burdened complete,
passed-on trauma, soul becomes invisible to the reality of personal
insignificance being helpless in emotionally flooding incomplete.

But why do I feel more insecure now than I did before I started this
deep delve?

The Lie

The lie that personal power is attached to is this: "Personal existence is
misfit at governing a subjective reality of self-importance, as she lacks
attunement with inferiority being the way of enabling codependency as
love and commitment to soul tie."

What keeps me down now?

35

FEELING GOOD

WHAT KEEPS ME DOWN IS a distressing of any commitment to positivity being visible in living. This has come up already so what exactly does this mean for me?

The brain distresses the mind opening up capacity to me feeling good about me and my life because of the effects it created in my primal years.

I numb my emotions. I am numb to the energy I give off. I am to numb positivity if I want to encourage a connection with others.

I am not aware of how I feel in any given moment. My mind races ahead of me when I put effort into something just for me such as art or rock climbing. I can't be in the moment and enjoy the process. I can't feel at home in my house because I can't attach to it being mine. I paint but I don't feel a sense of accomplishment or pride for doing something good for me and for what I have. I want someone else to do the work so that I can attach to the outcome with gratitude for a job that I can see and appreciate. I struggle with letting go in intimacy. My husband says that I control my intimate relationships. I go for hikes and when I am finished, my muscles tighten up and I feel really tired in mind. I talked this out with my husband and he said that my endorphins kick in when I do activity (actually, anything for myself) and my mind can't deal with feeling good and satisfied that it evokes so it shuts down from forming an awareness of the energy of positivity I act out. My mind distresses any commitment to output energy of positivity, as my right to do so was shut down from being visible in my reality of living as a young child.

And then a deeper truth comes to mind. I was controlled from coming into complete. I don't feel complete in my relationships because mom manipulated the attention away from me so I have never cemented love between my dad and me or my brothers and me (this has followed into adulthood). I am pained when my boys are indifferent with me but I in turn do it to my husband. I am indifferent to him acting out desire for me. Indifference is how we assert love-struck in my childhood.

Mom took away all the things I put attention to as she didn't want me to come into a sense of being complete for myself. I have a broken heart from love never forming complete attachments to me. And I lack certainty of knowing myself as I was shut down from lovingly attaching to my life having meaning. I discourage myself from being secure in my way on my own because existence has been about maturing negativity as the only way to focus on.

I put so much time and effort into showing care for my youngest, being indifferent with me, because I have been programmed to interconnect presence with self-scarcity. Right now I am committing positivity to suffering because of independence being denied autonomy over encompassing negativity as the only paradigm to pay attention to.

Intimacy has been blocked for so long that it has been committed to a concept which self wants me to easily walk away from when feeling betrayed, alone or disregarded.

36

MY HUSBAND

I WAS AT A TURNING point, needing a change. A counsellor had me write out all the qualities I wanted in a man. I kept that list for a quite a while. When I met my husband, he wasn't on my list, so he wasn't my kind but essence knew he would be good for me. I realized that the list was fluffy and had no substance so I threw it away.

Nine years ago when we moved into our second house, the "ugly" qualities started to show its face. My husband wouldn't help me with the youngest that shut the door to interacting with us. Everything was a struggle. I would yell at him that I wanted to hit him out of pure frustration but wouldn't because that wasn't love. He didn't seem to care. Son seemed to egg me on. I wanted to talk to understand what was going on but he clamped his mouth shut. My husband evaded the whole situation. My husband has never been on board with me to set rules and enforce consequences. He doesn't stand up for me. He says it's because I'm a strong woman that he doesn't feel the need to stand up for me. But boys learn how to become a man and how to treat a woman by their father showing them the way (or not).

Over the years, I have tried to talk this out with my husband but he deflects and puts the attention back on me, usually by saying something to the effect that it's my fault because I haven't had the role modelling to show me how to stay strong my way. Then he gives me suggestions on how to show more love to my son(s). My husband pours positivity over everything thinking that it heals all. But I am realizing that the energy of positivity is much different from the positivity of essence. By throwing positivity over negativity consistently, it has strengthened negativity to be the way that exists and garners attention. And if I don't garner the same attention towards negativity, then something is missing in me and I am the one that has to change. And it gets me second guessing myself (mind fucking) wondering where the love is.

My husband validates negativity's attributes as having more life than the true positivity traits I encompass. He does not acknowledge the true positivity of me or him. True positivity is truth, vulnerability, sincerity, and compassion.

I will share an example. The other night, the three of us were playing cards. At one point, I said to my boy that I was reflecting and realizing that I judge him. I mistook something he said earlier as him ganging up on me but what he was doing was challenging me with another alternative. I jumped to conclusions of judgment. Son looked pleasantly surprised that I was admitting this to him. My husband sat there, dissociating his presence with true positivity. He didn't say a word; nor did he mention it later. My dad was the same way; he poured positivity into activity with us kids but when he was needed to emotionally connect, he bowed out, often turning a blind eye and ear to what was happening. My dad doesn't truly see me, the complete me; and I believe my husband is the same way. Positivity of essence is out of awareness for them as they are disconnected from higher self.

And that is why essence knows my husband is good for me; he is demonstrating the same attributes of my dad that are staring me in the face to heal.

As for intimacy, I need a man who is not my dad. I need a man who can recognize that I am complete so I can freely, confidently and securely interconnect presence with self-truth (positivity) so that the scapegoat role will be banned forever. But is it really up to my husband to provide that for me? Why am I not doing this for myself? I know I am complete but the impact of not being seen most of my life has me helpless identifying complete as real in life. I need it to be validated that it is out of the shadow of scarcity and that will happen if my husband is vulnerable in accepting his part of the burdening of positivity. On my end, I can't keep taking the blame or holding myself responsible for my family's personal shut-down or awakening. On my husband's end, if he wants to be a partner of mine, he needs to get open with truth.

Self-inquire: self is anxious of "free will" (my choice) being vulnerable in keeping my husband around. I have actually been looking at options to gain independence; this isn't the first time. But the truth of me doesn't want that. How am I vulnerable by staying around? The injury from dad's blindness has self push back from my husband who is willing to pay attention to his part in the lack of harmony. He is agreeing to go to counselling; he said that he has wanted to but got sidetracked. He thanked me for the push. I know this is love on both sides. And most of us need the push because the mind will gravitate to safety; and safety isn't about looking at the pain to the mind that has been pained.

37

THE DARK FORCE

I AM TRYING TO FIGURE out what heaviness is trapping me; is it of me or is it not?

As I reflect on my life, I can see how I emotionally separate from all aspects of it, whether it is hiking out in the bush, making love with my husband or connecting with my children, I hold back as I perceive me to be a burden to existence in any given moment. Some force keeps bringing me into the state of being pained which brings about life as scarce in consciousness for me.

A thought came to me: as a soul tie couple, my husband and I control love-struck acting out complete to get "being loved and loving" right by the way it was conditioned to be in our childhoods. His way is hovering and fearful of not getting it right and my way is detaching and knowing that I will never get it right by the objective standard. Together, our interactions are wired for "pained" as it validates us incomplete in our expressions of being true to us and for each other.

My state of being (neutrality) demands that I only accept "perfect" because the pain of being consistently validated a mistake doesn't perceive another state other than shame.

I feel like I have to go back to the beginning and gain more clarity. This is hard work!

God is neutrality. The Holy Spirit I refer to is of God that is the spirit of the negative and the spirit of the positive. Human's neutrality is of both spirits but will attune more with the positive spirit of God (we know as real) or the negative spirit of God (we label and judge as who we are because of a sense of incomplete).

Adam and Eve

Eve was validated to be less than Adam, the sinner who manipulated "wrong" to be "right" by coaxing him to eat the apple. But Adam committed wrong judgment when he didn't discourage Eve in her independence in choosing as he didn't want to take responsibility for any downfall that was going to happen. Adam knew the consequences; Eve did not. We would judge Eve naïve but actually she was secure in her attunement with the positive while Adam was attuned to the negative. He had her trust which was used to encourage Eve to eat the apple. This collaboration between the positive interconnecting with the negative encouraged homeostasis as a maturing of incomplete; the negative interconnects with the positive as broken because the positive can't rely on the negative to redirect from any distress that comes their way to tear them apart. Their strength would have been in joining together; it's not in the insecurity that negativity attunes to which brings about separation through not standing up for beloved.

Negativity recognizes love in the form of judgment as it judges itself "shame."

I go back to thinking about a "Bachelorette" series that I got into watching a few years back. She fell for the "bad boy" quickly and through the dating series, he proved that he couldn't be there for her. He kept apologizing and she believed in him, taking him back. But there was one gentleman who was slow to get her attention and by the last few episodes, she was falling in love with him. But who got the last rose to be "the one?" The one who was helpless being mature in showing up for her got the last rose. Why did she pick him and not the reliable, mature, and emotionally available man? A lot of us go for what is comfortable, certain, and safe because we know it with our being; we have lived it and attune to it being the way that is to exist and take precedence.

My husband says there is a line of thought out there about women wanting the man who takes charge and forces his agenda onto her, which usually entails control in the bedroom. Well, that is the type this bachelorette picked and that is the type of man I picked before I got married. And yes, at the beginning I felt that my husband was boring, weak and insecure in loving me; that is so far from the truth. These mature in love men are grounded and certain of their feelings for us without games and dishonesty taking root. I became so much more open, sexualized and loving as I peeled the layers of inferiority back that held me captive.

The essence of self is not wired for pain or worldly gain; it is wired for feeling pleasure through the reciprocation of value(s).

Also, there is no such thing as "sin" that is referred to in the bible. There is no shame to the positive spirit or the negative spirit as they are both sides of a God that is complete. The negative spirit is what gets handed down from generation to generation as a state of existence that keeps being reinforced as the reality to mature.

Did you take this negative spirit on or did you not? I did not. But the state of neutrality (being) keeps pulling me into the shadow because of the abuse it endured in childhood. Neutrality is attuned to enforcing the negative side of childhood as existence because that was 100% of what I endured. The positive side of this (unconscious strength) is the faith I have in me and my tenacity to keep going down the positive track to governing superiority in bringing my existence to where it belongs which is in the light and love of complete. I was born with a mindset of self-importance and I am and always have been attuned to what is real and truthful.

My husband is on holidays and is talking this out with me. We are celebrating our twenty fifth anniversary next week and I go to him because he has been my witness for half my life. He knows me well; he has sat through a few suicidal episodes to keep me safe and has cheered me on as I started a business. He says that what caught his attention when I met him was me being open, joyful, loving, caring and free spirited. But he's noticed that when people try to attach to me, I clam up and become serious in nature. It's like love-struck is dangerous for me. The more we talked, the more something was rising to the surface for me. I am wondering what the space is between me being me and all seems fine, to me being me but the males treat me different and mom is mean to me. What happened in the interim? What happened is the transitioning from mom not noticing me to mom noticing all the attention I was getting from all the males. For me, existing became anything that was contrary to love-struck which meant a separation of self from forming a commitment to self-love and life.

It is hard for me to admit that I was out to get mom's approval to prove me not the lie that she was enforcing as her truth. Existing for me has been to separate myself from her but I have also been divided from essence when in the energy of competence in connecting to love.

My husband commented that I negate, bury, or forgive harm done to me. Why do I do that without thought to it? It's because I acknowledge being shut down as the structure to how I should exist. I am assuming the objective or the negative mind as my existence, my mind. My mind resists what the essence of me wants because existing cannot attune to the positivity of aligning with the light of me.

And then the lightbulb went on when I was driving home. My husband has a lot of fear; I have never thought that I did. But I must! We are both fearful of being rejected from others when they see that our value holds no promise of connection. He hides in the shadows and doesn't stand up for his worth; nor does he stand up too negativity. I easily put myself out there and stand up to negativity but I realize that I don't speak up for myself; I speak up for those that are weak in using their voice and I hold compassion for those who "unknowingly" harm me. Why? Giving to selfishness/ narcissism but not getting back is what I have attuned to as the appropriate way to exist- it's about shutting me down from forming an actual healthy relationship because that was never appropriate for me to do.

While we were walking back from getting groceries, I had a talk with my husband about our boys and how we have been smothering them with fear rather than challenging them with persistent competence in taking steps forward. When we got home and unpackaged the food, my husband got on the phone and looked up some ideas for the middle boy. In a split second, my shoulders and neck muscles constricted and head started spinning. I had to sit down when anxiety rose up so I wouldn't faint standing up. But I didn't faint. I just felt nauseous. What happened is that I got triggered by my husband taking the initiative to follow up on a need for change that I expressed. I was expecting anxious despondence that he used to give me and not the mature availability that I was now getting from him. This shows me how strong our inner coping mechanisms can be in shutting down to perceiving another viewpoint and recognizing another different way that is possible. We are often one track minded.

Damaged: inflict harm on someone so as to impair their value which would then function as "the lie/ dark side/ sin' broken/ contrary to true self."

It is hard to get a clear answer when I muscle test because subjectivity is denying being damaged because of my power to bring about first impressions (this is when essence shines freely). But if subjectivity denies the damage, that means it is actually depriving "real" from governing an honest relationship with self and others. Put another way, if I am not being awake to how I have been schooled to self-destruct, then I am blind to

1. how I deprive myself a reality in which people assume the best of me all of the time and
2. how superiority gets constricted by the existence of self-destruct.

The dark force is manipulating my mind to fail/ self-destruct this restoring of self that I am doing by reinforcing autonomy to fail at believing that I am structuring a state of existing as value even if I can't see it. I can't see God but I know God exists. Just because I am not attuned with the changes I am creating doesn't mean that I am not making progress.

What does value honestly mean in this context? Value is being real. For me, real is a governing of self-importance as a paradigm of nurturing a belief that I exist, loved, in the energy of God.

The dark force waits for its opportunity to shut the mind down from assuming an existence of value. It happened to me when mom separated from us and dad shut down from paying attention to me.

Being shut-down was the structured mindset that I needed to adhere to. Existing is not attuned to being compatible with essence.

It seems that it is my mind that is resisting what the essence of me wants because I keep getting these frontal headaches when I come into an awareness of what it is I truly want for myself. But I am realizing that on some unexplained level, existing cannot attune to the positivity of aligning with the light of me. Why not?

I think my answer is with the shame of Adam. How did Adam in the garden not stand by Eve in his attunement with negativity? Where would he learn to judge love? How did shame get attached to him? Where did this sense of shame arise from? Because I believe this source of shame through judgment is what is trapping me in scarcity.

The serpent/ devil/ trickster/ dark force enforces distress as existence. This entity is attached to the negative side of God but is separate in its governance of forcing competence in helplessness with love.

The power of the D.F.

I am at work eating my cauliflower and my client asks me what I am doing because she can hear this swishing sound coming from me. I said I am moving my cauliflower around in my container as I eat. All of a sudden, something hard that I can't bite through appears in my mouth. I take it out and notice that it is a piece of glass. A few bites later and another piece of glass shows up in my mouth. What the heck, as I did not see them in the container; there is no way I could have missed them. I took a picture of them and sent it to husband who asked the boys if any glass had broken recently. Nothing was broken.

I asked my celestial team if it is a miracle and the answer that came up is "God creates miracles; dark force creates cruel intentions to injure."

The glass represents the D.F. embedding into my life so I don't become complete by finishing and distributing this book. It is forcing injury towards me growing complete. It creates confusion to my mind as to why my life is not changing by me growing complete. It is disabling an impact of my growth actually creating massive change in our world.

Personally, I need to not react to injury which is me giving attention to the force disabling me. What do I do with the force disabling me? I need to grow what I am good at and what I enjoy to do. I need to finish this book and hand it over. Will it be able to be distributed with this force at play? Yes. How? Privilege; immunity will be granted by God of light when I let the book go.

How that word "privilege" triggers me. White privilege, spewing of racism and sexual orientation labelling affect me so as the expressions are used incorrectly and inappropriately. But when I say something about it, I am called a racist. This is all the D.F. trying to distract humans from the true cause that needs attending to and that is getting back to truth. Simply put, the truth is we are all value.

Value

This world resides in a clash of values. For me, the value of self is about equality in neutrality but this has me in conflict with the anxious attackers whose value of self is a paradigm of inferiority, division, and class rating. Even my boys laugh at me and challenge my notion that we are of the same value because of what they see on social media. There is a lack of sensitivity from the majority because there is a focus of selfish absorption. But these people are hiding from their inner insecurity they feel when internalizing value that is the real self. (They turn away from the deepest truth within.)

The goal of the D.F. is to shut superiority down from aligning with value to validate oneself complete in their existence. What exactly is complete? It is about portraying essence of self in the positive, committed to non-judgment of labelling living beings, standing up to negativity taking over, encouraging an interconnecting essence with love and autonomy over fulfilling one's own purpose for being here.

Expressing complete for me is that I have the ability to perceive the righteousness over negativity and am willing to stand up for it.

The way to live true to self is to encompass and empower a belief that existence of all living beings are attuned to value as a paradigm of being real. Yes, there is a division of wealth and power but in value there should be no poorness of starvation. In the structure of governing value as one's own truth, we would be empowered to follow through with a collective effort to govern a personal autonomy over one's own existence. Should the giver expect something in return? No; to expect in return is to shut-down to attaching to an assumption that one's value is important to its autonomy with personal power being on the inside of value. Value is being able to stand tall with no insisting upon proving self is value.

Value is not tangible; it's a characteristic of existing in a paradigm of real. Real is a mindset that functions subjectively in following through, attuned with value, as a way to nurture one's power to be.

I have been regarding neutrality as essence but they aren't the same. Neutrality is being; being alive and real. Essence attunes to neutrality as value and empowers a follow through with autonomy over value existing. Value, as a characteristic of neautrality, is being exposed as a paradigm of real, but real is shut-down from acknowledging that it is being deprived of structuring autonomy over its existence. How? The mind of helpless resigns real to the fact that it gets damaged when following through with autonomy over its existence so it makes sure that real doesn't contribute to existing as a belief that it exists subjective in nature.

In helplessness, the mind unknowingly partners with the D.F. to shut real down from existing as value; the D.F. deprives a structuring of me nurturing subjectivity as an entity that is alive and well.

The shadow that reinforces shut-down to value's existence is the mind being helpless in connecting subjectivity with value; the helplessness has to do with inferiority. My mind is insecure existing aligned, sovereign in value, due to the mind attuned to its environment creating me an inferior entity. My mind is being shut down from recognizing that the rest of me is attaching to an assumption of being value. The mind, trying to bond, has the D.F. influence insecurity in my attachments. What is this insecurity? I am anxious to nurture a boundary of value being included in spaces where there is lots of insecurities and helplessness. What is the anxiety? I am anxious of expressing self-value and it being forced to break down to be included in conversations of collaborations; just as my mom did with me. (Good to know this. I know I hold back from sharing my value in group contact as I am on guard of value being deprived attaching. Knowing why, I can enforce the D.F. into the shadow.) What should an attachment entail? An attachment should entail an attunement with the value of bonding with like values.

Oh! I get it. Like values has always been an obstacle for me to attune to because I was shut-down from embracing them from others as a part of my reality that I want to exist by. I am recognizing that I can tell that I am opening up consciousness to my values as I have approached people that are not normally the type I would gravitate to. And my food, I want it to taste good so I will put my money towards that which makes my taste buds dance. And I just painted the kitchen with my husband and changed a few things around to suit my creative side. I am putting up fairy lights and placing cherubs around as they make my energy feel energized.

I am still experiencing pain and discomfort in multiple forms, so I keep inquiring.

The Duality of Self

I have a boundary of complete within that is innately subjective.

I have paradigms of incomplete within that come from attuning with the objective. Paradigms are most often an imprinting on one's energetic field.

My being was shattered by the main paradigm of needing subjective to be non-existent; it deprived my boundary of complete an existence. This is why it is so difficult for me to bring up the truth within as my brain and mind have disconnected associating with the truth of me.

Moving on,

The matriarchal meme as life: to be forced into shutting down complete being innocent in its existence.

The patriarchal meme as life: to not stand mature in offering support against this shut-down, forces complete into existing as a paradigm of inferiority and a boundary of "pained".

Together, it influences me to internalize that following through with living will get shut-down by those who constrict accountability in establishing a sense of safety surrounding personal existing.

Safety: establishing space for the practice of shutting down any effort that follows through with constricting real, subjectively recognizing, learning, engaging, contributing and experiencing self and life.

The people who play out paradigms of anxiety, self-absorption, regression and narcissism typically do not take responsibility in their part of controlling love. They are busy nurturing a false satisfaction of existing in their pretend world of control (lost in addictions, screen time, alone time, depression, close-mindedness, religions, politics and war). Then there are others who, in their anxiety of what has happened to them in the past, don't stand up to loved ones repressing their value because they are trying to protect them from existing being pained. They are taking the space of learning from natural and logical consequences away because of blindness to their own pained existence influencing a nurturing of repression.

As a child, my acts of self-determination were kept quiet and personal to keep persecution away. When I was around others, I numbed my energy, matching my competence to be what others needed me to be. When mom left, I had space to breathe. I thought it to be my time to live my life on my terms; but dad and brothers were distressed and showed weakness in addictions. I held back, knowing it wasn't right to put myself first because the need of the weakened needed the space to utilize their own autonomy. This is playing out with my clients and two sons at home- I am giving them a false sense of bonding when I repress my energy to match theirs. Repression is what superiority has come to mean for me.

Repression is both the act of subduing someone and the restraint, prevention, or inhibition of subjectivity.

I am going to truly work on identifying the root of this repression because it isn't as easy as identifying a belief or managing my emotions. I am going back to my own notes on the brain.

Part of the brain, called the hippocampus, releases the hormone cortisol when stress is triggered. Stress is the energy of subjectivity moving into the light. My brain's structure, regulating cortisol when my energy gets revved up, stops a belief of being safe attaching to life. The belief being shut-down from proceeding constricts the amygdala, the part of the brain associated with restoring follow through, inflaming neurotransmitters regulating my energy. A lack of oxygen to these neuro transmitters constricts personal power in self-governing value. A brain that has been deprived energy of showing love, represses following through with living because validating love a part of life has been scarce in presence. This scarcity commits the brain to "less than". The brain stem commits self-competence as danger, shutting down the energy of personal power that has the ability to restore value.

Anxiousness comes from amygdala assuming existence to be dangerous, due to the brain stem pressuring autonomy's existence to be scarce in existing.

Through repression, autonomy commits life to a will that needs to be met. What is your will? Autonomy is my will to commit love to life.

Existing is anxious attaching while living is a belief of being value.

Value is an established energy from the beginning of time. Yes, you are a conceived energy of value before you become a physical reality. God intends the energy of value to follow through with attuning to superiority to intend an empowered "real" which is the incarnate- spirit of God attached to each of our energy of value, to live life in human form as an entity of being physically on the inside of love. Being shut-down from following through attuning to superiority, deprives our attachment with God a belief that we exist, interconnected, being on the inside of love. Our physical existence is intended to encompass superiority, which is our energy of value, a place on the inside with Beloved.

How do I encourage homeostasis as life and living Trinity of Jesus, Holy Spirit of God, and autonomy/will of value (Father)? I need to interconnect presence with love; but I am struggling with this because of my brain being committed to scarcity. My brain is deprived experiencing positivity being projected at me as an acceptance of me being real.

Everything is cerebral with me.

And then life happened to me.

My daughter did a zoom call with me to go over something that I asked her to do plus we try to keep in touch monthly. I try to end the conversation with her when I have to share of myself. But on this call, she kept encouraging the conversation to go forward. We got in deep. I shared what is going on with me at the moment and how I believe it influences her existence. I talked about the vortex of negativity that suffocates my existence and she said she feels it; that's why she had to leave the city. She told me when she came back for the holidays last year, and snow storms kept her here for a couple more days, she was feeling the effects of this vortex squeezing her. She said that I was even part of the negativity.

I asked her how I played into the negativity.

She said "It seems sometimes like you don't see me as me. You would say contradicting things because I know you support me but you would question my projects, studies and criticize my appearance."

I have told her that at that time, I couldn't see me so I couldn't see her but that I am healing this duality of self. While we got deeper in the conversation, I was commenting that she is a lot like me. I also recognized that I am blind to my past and the participation of negativity while she is quite aware of it. She says that she can actually hear the voice that isn't hers and she can identify who it belongs to. I have learned to numb my experience of being in the moment with myself and my stress.

I got off the call and went to eat some cereal. Over my bowl, a huge wave of emotion hit and I sat there and cried.

Then my husband and youngest son came in the door after having done an errand. I said it was bad timing. My husband said it looked like the right timing. He came over to give me a hug. I had stopped crying but the emotion was brimming underneath still. My husband starts spreading his positivity through storytelling and my son starts his poking at me. I finally turned to them and said, "Husband, I don't need you to slather positivity on this and son, shut up because I don't need you attacking my femininity." All got quiet; I started to cry over my cereal again.

Then it dawned on me what happened during my conversation with my daughter.

I was validated.

My daughter mirrored the vortex of negativity so I know it isn't just my experience. Plus, she mirrored the truth of me. I saw me through her. Actually, it is more about seeing me as an existence. I actually do exist as a denied vision I have had about myself. I am value and always have been. We are both lone females in a sea of masculine anxiousness attaching to us because we know who we are deep inside but struggle showing it out there and having it accepted.

My brain's hippocampus perceives my husband as stress because it doesn't have a structure that holds positive intentions towards me. This part of the brain is attuned to stress of youngest son as that is what consisted as the vortex in my developing years. The vortex consists of parents, grandparents, uncles, aunts, cousins and priests that came to the school. With that much "shut down to love" enveloping me, no wonder my brain protects against something that is on the outside of this vortex which is positive intentions towards me and seeing me for who I am.

I sent a text to my daughter sharing the gift of our extended talk. She said I probably understood her experience when she voiced it was because I was also the only girl with three brothers, who felt invisible being the only girl. That's put simply; but that is what triggered me. She said she is glad she is starting to really recognize what is going on so we can talk it out. I am more than glad too. This is what I have tried to nurture between my mom and me but her brain can't open up to me being sincere in my communication.

All of the jobs I have taken on, or all the relationships I have invested in, have never experienced the full capacity of what I am capable of doing because following through with a belief that I exist as value has always been experienced as repression to the mind. The repression of autonomy has lacked the power to realize subjective innocence in my effort to bring me forward as the ego perceives there is danger through the focus of duality. My whole cerebral system shuts down superiority gaining ground on attaching autonomy to experiencing its value in existing.

I need to go for a walk to have the answer I seek come up. Before I leave, my husband mentioned a couple of things that he has noticed about me. First, that I had a dewy look on my face when I held my daughter and youngest son as babies. Second, that my daughter would get prissy at me at sixteen like my youngest is doing with me and she got me just as anxious in her presence as he is doing now in my presence.

On my walk a revelation hits.

My brain commits the energy of my family as it relates to the energy of my childhood family of origin. Here is how it plays out:

1. My oldest son is like my father who does for everyone else, has a couple of drinks when needing soothing, puts his head in the sand around narcissism, doesn't really have a true sense of self, yet wants freedom in himself and still be connected to his loved one.

2. My daughter is represented in the context of mother-daughter relationship being shut-down to subjective existing.

3. My youngest son represents the vortex of my childhood origin. Both my daughter and youngest son challenge my sincerity.

4. My middle boy represents an anxious void belonging which is like me.

5. My husband represents my dad. But what the brain doesn't recognize is that my husband regards me with sincerity and sees the real me. My brain or my mind does not know sincerity so they don't recognize that it could be love that my husband has for me.

6. The people on the outside, my brain judges them committed to negativity (because no one supported me in my childhood and young adulthood showed me power struggles in leadership).

I had a dream that was stating that I don't allow presence my essence to live.

Then I went to a reflexology session and had most spots on my feet feel sensitive which goes with parts of my body or internal systems such as digestion and lymph nodes and my spine and brain.. Am I always on alert? Then the words "on guard" came to consciousness. I am on guard with the paradigm of negativity perceiving me …….. Nothing comes up. Maybe that's it. It feels to my brain, mind, heart and body that everything about my human existence has been saturated with negativity; all because that is what I absorbed in the womb which became my experience post womb.

The womb was deprived a sense of self, positivity, life and love. Then what did I reference me as because I have no idea or specific thought about it; it's like a void in a blurry mind. I talk it out with my husband and the words *"negative asset"* comes to mind.

Negative Asset: I did not have value, quality or usefulness being me. My will to be me apart from my surroundings was repressed by being acknowledged as....... the word "critical" comes up. I look up the word and realize that I was not allowed to express my internal workings of mind and emotions and I wasn't involved in analysis of the merits and faults of my upbringing as no one seemed to want to acknowledge what was really going on.

Nothing seemed real to me. In this void of real, I am insecure of identifying with anything specific, especially if it doesn't fit the mold. This brain/mind of insecurity projects as an idea that has been shut-down from existing in less-real. My view is that everyone and everything is tinged by less-real. Real is someone giving me space to regard my existence the way my will to be me wants to, at all times. My will knows what I am capable of and what I am competent in doing. But who can maturely handle being in that energy of mine? To start with, my husband can.

Hopeless

I am hopeless attaching presence with will. I have the will to push forward but I numb associating my value as the energy conductor because I don't associate presence with being real. My childhood being void of real constricted the presence of real being free and safe to experience her essence. My energy isn't the positivity of self-assurance; it's the energy of negativity's anxiousness in attaching presence with the paradigm of un-real.

I assume following through with putting me out there to contribute has no support to attach to which leaves me deprived of existing. I often feel deflated, talked-over and ignored when I do try to start up a relationship of mutual intention; it's a focus to showcase them than build presence of personal power on the same footing of innate value. But then this is what I attract into my circle because "the void" is anxious to nurture something outside of the paradigms that my brain/mind recognizes as a mindset of existing.

Oh! I get it.

My existence never being validated real holds a void where a belief of real should be. And real can't show up because it doesn't exist to the circle.

How do I implement a belief of real?

I need to attach presence with the will that is progressing subjective existing. I do this by internalizing the attention I put towards existing, as the subjective, structuring a new reality for real.

38

PAINED

WHEN JESUS WAS CRUCIFIED, DARKNESS fell over the land. Darkness represents the dark force trying to shut-down life for the king's rising. Darkness is associated with shut-down (evil), hopelessness, despair and scarcity. The king rising represents energy progressing autonomy over death of the human experience. It wasn't a physical body coming back to life; it was an energetic power, having always existed as value.

Jesus has power over the paradigm of darkness that seems to have a real attachment to being established a boundary of value. But paradigms are not value. "Innocence of the sacred heart of Jesus" is value.

Jesus is the bridge between humanity and heaven. Heaven knows the innocence of Jesus as beloved and his attunement with superiority as his relationship with humanity.

The thought struck me that Jesus had no male model impregnating him into life; but then he didn't have a female one either, even though he was born from the womb. Jesus is born a boundary of value, attuned with his heavenly father, God and nurtured by mother Mary's attachment to innocence.

Adam and Eve's influence of pained (lacking a united force of living out value) influences impending generations to exist through the same paradigm. Adam passes on a *rationalizing* of pained while Eve passes on a *compensating* for the pained. We can see this played out everywhere! Sure, culture and tradition might be different in areas of the world but all around the world, the same division exists between the man and the woman.

Jesus came to undo the rationalizing and compensating from the dark force's satisfaction with watching the play out of our disjointedness.

We need to recognize how this darkness triggers pained so that we can shut-down this influence from assuming follow through with existing as real in each of our lives.

Fuck, I am in pain.

Is it really a dark force that resides outside of me? This is what I am actually suspicious about. I think the pained mind is so strong that it can bring into reality anything that will validate love-struck is being controlled; the *mind of paradigms* forbids a *mind of consciousness* from knowing what acting out love-struck would actually bring about. I have dissension between minds going on here!

I go to cuddle with my husband. We always have great conversations in bed but I didn't realize why until now.

1st: he cultivates the conversation around me. I now realize that he deflects attention away from himself to support me.

2nd: by talking things out with him, I am allowed to word vomit until an A-Ha strikes me.

3rd: it builds intimacy. My husband feels privileged in being my sounding board; and I get closer to him when he listens to me.

4th: I feel validated when he listens and puts effort into making me feel good. I have had pleasure with previous relationships but for the most part, have never felt lovable. Or maybe I had the wall up to a man showing me that I am lovable so he didn't stand a chance staying with me.

I looked to my husband and said "I think you deflect because your mind believes that you aren't lovable." It's only taken us twenty five years to figure this out. I think the sanctity of marriage is breaking down because people haven't been validated lovable by the one they need validation from.

6th: expressing who I am to my husband grows a belief that there is something right with me when he connects to this repressed knowing of self being value.

Associating with the energy of subjectivity is still being closed down. I am heavy, tight and sore. I am getting frustrated with stating this. Jesus, what is going on? Is it my mind? No. Is it a force? Yes. Again, is it mine or outside of me? I want to take responsibility for my pain!

I go to bed and dream. In the morning my husband comes in to cuddle with me. I tell him the dream; he said it sounds like the male influence is always there in the background, invisible, but still deeply impacting my life. Yes, and it keeps being played out; I just need to identify exactly what is being played out.

I had an incident with my son one night and the next day when I go to tell my husband about it, he said that he had an incident with him too when I was at work. I talked out my husband's trigger and then listened to a story he heard from a friend. The word "*tortured*" came up and I knew that is how I feel inside. We went to cuddle. But while in bed, I sat up near tears. I asked him how he can easily brush off what was said about his trigger and I can't. I can't because all my mind associates bonding as is torture. But why hasn't my mind associated with being tortured?

Since I wasn't allowed to speak or show emotions, my mind shut-down to identifying them. How I am feeling, how I perceive things, what I have accomplished, what people have said about me does not come up to consciousness and when essence brings it to consciousness, it will not stay put! I have to ask my husband what was said again or tap into his memory as he knows all the stories about me. And then it dawns on me; this is being a void.

Once I talked this out with my husband, I was able to relax the mind by breathing and paying attention to him stroking my skin. Such a soothing yet tantalizing feeling; I love experiencing tingles. I can let go of the mind when he focuses his love onto me. Why can't I focus on me and not have the mind turn on me? My mind tortures me trying to live as though I am more than a void.

My mind is helpless validating me complete in any expression of getting it right because the energy of "who am I to...." triggers a void, which has my mind certain that real doesn't exist. What void came from expressing "who am I to..."? The void is "being real is made to be shamed for being innocent in my regard of self." I was created "contrary" which is something or someone that I am not but have been validated to be (selfish, insensitive, unlovable, slut and a disdained "who do you think you are acting like you are significant Athena"). This tears away at my energy to move up and forward because this way of treating me was passed onto my younger sons. I am stuck in it as my mind regresses into helplessness instead of the know-how to solve dissension.

This state of being matures because it hasn't become clear as to what needs to be fixed.

To Reconcile

To bring self into harmony by making consistent acting out superiority regarding love-struck, I need to control the triggering of pained by focusing on my breath and reaffirming my value has the power to deny enveloping sadness the satisfaction of regressing.

Feels like sadness but shame envelops the void. Shame shuts down certainty that I was born to grow a family by me loving them. The males in my life do not know what they are missing from not engaging with me in love-struck. I certainly experience the pain of it every day. What I shouldn't be doing is beating myself up by being the blame. Shame took over my humanly existence, opening up the will (the belief that I have the right to exist amongst invisibility) to therapy (I am a problem because I want to exist in real). This makes for a very lonely existence; only because my mind won't attach to beloved.

My mind stays helpless in beloved growing a validation that I have always belonged as I am the one, who in love, created this family to be, whether or not we can acknowledge each other's value as real. Why does it stay helpless? The void controls restoring an existence of real because an existence of real was and still is perceived bullied to the outside of belonging.

My husband asks me if I really want a real communion with him or do I need the strife to feel alive. That's been the problem; I have never been able to acknowledge to myself that I deserve more and that I know how to create that more when I see it. I married him because I intuitively knew I could have more. With consistent love for me and growing maturity to becoming real apart from his own control in love-struck, my husband is helping me create a whole mindset regarding self-value and love. I've always had a mindset of value which encompasses a knowing to forming healthy connections; it just hasn't been validated real to the mind-set shut-down to love, until now.

39

THE CAUSE

A TITLE ON PINTEREST CAUGHT my eye; it was about hormones, menopause and healthy therapies. I muscle tested to see if any of these therapies could help my aches and pains but what came up is that I have to look at my energy; my energy is inflamed.

The will to restore love-struck provokes the *lifeline of deprivation* (the void), intensifying its withholding of energy that powers superiority restoring value's existence.

Lifeline of deprivation: a structured paradigm of emptiness. This paradigm controls superiority nurturing the truth of me into existence, as the truth was established to be inferior to the power that keeps me down. What exactly is this power that keeps me down and in the shadow? The power that keeps me down is the scarring of deprivation that numbs and tunes out real existing.

Emotional numbing is the mental and emotional process of shutting down superiority restoring self-value. This can be experienced as self-sabotage, responding based on what energy is projected at you, suppressing maturely responding to emotion because of controlling superiority (the energy of self).

Tuning out is constricting awareness of the real me structuring intentions to get help and nurture bringing real up and into the light.

So, I can see that there are a few descriptions coming up for the same thing but have yet to figure out what this exact thing is. Lifeline of deprivation, the void, contrary, tortured- what do they all represent? Value has always been non-existent so to have my energy restore something that was validated non-existent is war against what was validated real which is "nothing". What was validated value was actually false and contrary to my truth. But what needs to be validated is that anything apart from value is actually nothing. Value is real. Contrary is not.

❦ ❦ ❦

Something is not allowing me to attach to the truth that comes up for me. I think the unreal sure has its grips on me. But then if there is no such thing as the unreal being real, then what rhyme am I talking about here?

The truth is that there is a dark force that has the power to attack my mind from following through with establishing my existence on the inside of love. This dark force is my male's' insecurity in restoring value which makes me anxious to attach to value because insecurity contributes to duality - I can't be free being me if the males (dad and brothers, husband and sons) are insecure in being true to self. Why not? Attending to autonomy means I forsake restoring independent subjectivity for the sake of the males' insecure energy being revived. How is their energy more important to revive? My energy has always been shut-down for the objectifying of subjectivity; this has been my sovereignty.

As I input my notes onto the computer, the screen freezes and I have to shut the system down. The time it freezes at is 3:33. The spiritual meaning of 3:33 for me is that I becoming a Master that has established a respective belief that attaching to the inside of love brings up value from the shadow of deprivation.

Freedom

Awakening my mind to this objectifying of subjectivity will open me up to following through with autonomy over attaching subjectivity to existing as value.

Inside of love has come up a couple of times- "we exist, interconnected, being on the inside of love. Our physical existence is intended to encompass superiority, which is our energy of value, a place on the inside with Beloved."

What exactly does this mean for me/us?

Beloved interconnects as value - this connection is made when we attach to assuming value through a belief of existing on the inside of heaven in partnership with being human. Heaven is found here on earth, played out in superiority attuned to living real.

I thought I would lighten up but my energy is heavier than it has ever been.

I muscle test to see what it could be about and found that it has to do with deprivation, more specifically, *the energy that influences deprivation.*

The energy of Eve: overcompensating

It is a mind set on shutting down acknowledging the undoing of love-struck. How is it set? The split pained the play out of believing in self-importance. This made way for the dark force to claim our personal power, making it insecure in following through with superiority. We have become insecure in believing that our existence is approved of which projects "I am invisible" when we believe self-importance govern existing as value.

What exactly is the split that happened in the womb?

The state of being within the womb is "suicidal". The subjective mind of value gets imprinted with the inherited state of overcompensating; this creates autonomy to be suicidal, meaning a split outside the womb. The subjective gets shut-down by the state of overcompensating making us deprived of attaching to value which makes us invisible in existing.

Invisibility follows through with burdening superiority (the energy of self-progression) which is a state of suicidal. So true, as the more I try to move forward and the more nothing happens, the more suicidal I feel.

The biggest complaint I heard from my mom was being invisible to dad and "just his wife with no name" to his friends.

The energy of Adam: rationalizing

The males being insecure in following through with assuming power over the play out of forbidding an existing of self-value, shuts me down from nurturing my own existence of value. Why? I am acknowledged as a mind set on existing as a slave to their need to be nurtured through their addiction within the power struggle for existence. (My youngest son says I am here to serve him.) I rationalize that their lack of assuming power over their pain is because I haven't done enough to attach to them so I repress subjectivity to gain an attachment by serving them.

I nurture through being repressed. Not believing that I exist as value is energized to exist; so to my mind of deprivation, nurturing is repressing subjectivity having value outside of this void. But I rationalize this as me being lovable to everyone as I see everyone as value; but this is me controlling pained.

I rationalize my freedom. My freedom is only allowed if I disappoint the acting out of being satisfied with my life. I bring about pain on myself – distance myself from husband's attention, mother my boy's anxiety, prove myself sincere to youngest son, and don't phone my friends up – to stop feeling good vibes because that would show me that I actually do exist. Pained is my relationship with myself and others. What is normal to my state of being is to shut-down to love because normalcy growing up was experienced as pained.

My state of being is willing the energy of engagement to attach to my husband but the mind of deprivation constricts the energy that is bringing love to the light. Why? To the mind, this energy of love is known as suicidal.

I just heard that mom and youngest brother are planning on moving back home. This is not what I want at all but realize that it's coming full circle. I should be able to be the one who knows how to be the light in the darkness. I told my girlfriend about it and she said I can set my boundaries this time around our interactions. But I wonder how I can set boundaries with others when my own boundary of self is constricted from being.

How am I constricted in being?

My mind has no structure for love; thus, it has no structure for me.

My heart has been deprived of expressing itself as love because it was shamed for being a focus of contrary to the hate. It pains the mind to come into an identity as the mind only associates with energy that shames "contrary". I question if I am my mom because I have no certainty of existing respectively; I am a void. If I inquire into who I am contrary comes up.

What exactly is contrary?

I know contrary to mean opposite in nature; and I have finally come to terms to recognizing that I am nothing like the women in my lineage. But when I look up contrary online, as soon as I see the second definition of "perversely inclined to disagree", I knew I hit on something that I hadn't considered before.

I know the energy of following through has come up a lot but I haven't thought of body language and emotional flooding as a play out of energy. As a child, I didn't understand what was happening but I knew it didn't feel good to me. Looks of disdain, attitudes of hate, bitterness, behaviors of jealousy, and passive-aggressiveness were expressions that became a part of my everyday reality. They were not subjective but they were projected onto me to be subjective in the role of blame to shame and scapegoat. All these play out of energies were not only contrary to my innate energetic makeup, but they were what I experienced when I showed up being "perversely inclined".

I was given the impression that I was being perverse when I showed up as me. When I finally realized that it wasn't about me, that mom was being the mean one, I did show a deliberate and obstinate desire to behave in a way that was unreasonable as it was unacceptable to have me show up, especially opposing her and I needed to change that. I just wish that there would have been back-up to support me in that stance for myself.

I had emotionally shut-down recognizing what felt good to me and what didn't; as a result, it's been a struggle to emotionally attach as love to my soul tie. This journey is opening my mind up to the truth that I am uniquely me in such a positive way.

Having this come up must have made an inner shift because I am acting satisfied with associating me in relation to my husband. My husband is noticing as he said to me "Athena is back and I like it." Then he asks me if we are connecting more wholly because I feel safe with him, and I say it's something like that. It's about me recognizing that a space is being created where I can be authentic, open and receiving while noticing him just as is he is without trying to make him into something else.

We are different but working towards the same outcome which is love; something that didn't happen in my developing years. I am also recognizing that my communication with my sons is getting more real as I will admit when I am being too sensitive and judgmental and I can accept that their way doesn't need to be a certain way for us to attach. There is value in our differences. Yet opening my mind to this has my mind hurting (headache). And maybe it's because no matter what I do on my end to shift the mode of attaching, it doesn't seem to change much on my son's end. I get the same despondent attitude.

I can feel energy surge through me and it feels like hopelessness and anxiety. Something tells me that it's deeper like agony.

It is agony to interact with this world and have others notice me expressing complete because something harsh happens that has complete validate impaired but express as helpless.

- Impaired is the intake of *the significance of being wholly loved.* There is so much depth, meaning and sadness to these words for me which makes it hard to wrap my brain around this.
- Helpless is acting broken so I don't have to experience getting injured when I act out complete.
- Something harsh that happens is that the whole of me acts helpless in existing.

Mothering helplessness doesn't allow me to perceive the reality that I am expressing complete in any given moment.

What exactly is this helplessness that I keep mothering my existence by?

Helplessness is Toxicity.

Toxicity's definition by MedicineNet: the degree to which a substance (a toxin or poison) can harm humans or animals. ... Chronic toxicity is the ability of a substance or mixture of substances to cause harmful effects over an extended period, usually upon repeated or continuous exposure, sometimes lasting for the entire life of the exposed organism.

It becomes clear to me: mothering helplessness in attaching to my children because of a lack of touch that validates all is okay with me. I am able to get close to my husband now because I allow myself to transcend above my humanly constrictions when I get lost in his loving touch. My children don't reach out to hug me. My youngest son won't allow me to touch him. My childhood was deprived of a loving touch and a loving word that would validate me loveable which I reinforce as my reality with my own children because I perceive that it's me that is the trauma.

What's significant for me?

It is significant to validate that I grow complete through an important need of having loved ones attach to me. Attachment needs touch. Having the mother and the males detach from the realness of me in my childhood ingrained a *denied-avoidant attachment pattern* as a structure to exist by. My boys tease me that I am too sensitive around them and their disposition but what I am truly sensitive about is the energy of unlovable. The back of my mind holds this deep seated belief that I cause the family to treat me unlovable because of me expressing complete, which has me shame my efforts, but the truth is that expressing complete is validated toxic to those who don't express love back to me.

Expressions of unlovable are uncontrollable (helpless) to me being complete as these expressions have imprinted trauma into my energy receptors (that's why my whole body is tight). Being inundated with expressions of unlovable on a daily basis triggers being unloved in childhood; this impacts certainty that I will never get *the significance of being wholly loved* imprinting to be a validation of me being complete.

Thank God this is changing for me. And with all things, a focus of intention, which would be love of self, is needed to grow it into what I want it to be.

🦋 🦋 🦋

For my own sanity, this is where this book has to end. I have cracked the code on our existence and have gotten back to love. Obviously, with life being complex, there are a lot more topics that I have started to explore such as the relationship with COVID 19, racism, abortion, heaven and hell, transgender, individual purpose.... that I want to include in my next book.

40

IN CONCLUSION

FINALLY!

Patience has been my virtue.

This has been the most exhausting, drawn-out examination to get to the deepest of the deep within me so that I could resurrect my self. But I am grateful for this chance to have been the one to learn this technique and use it in confidence of my celestial team empowering me along the way of truth.

In an ideal, optimistic way of belonging, we would arrive into the world as lovable. After much reflection, lovable is defined as "self-expression being certain of being approved of being complete."

We would know ourselves as being important, and we would contribute to the unfolding of life as an adventure of expressing the true self into fulfillment. As family, we would each support the tribal members in their individual expression, naturally trusting that we would be uplifted in how we imagine our lives to become. Each person would instinctively feel safe to express and discover in their unique way of perceiving. We would assume only the best of ourselves and for ourselves, only accepting that which respects our values and personal truths.

I have learned that what we perceive to be value is where our attention and action follow. If negativity becomes value for us, then that is what we would attune to as being reality, and that is what we would recognize and accept into our lives as the way it should be. We would become helpless in creating healthy habits for our well-being, as we wouldn't hold value for them. We would also be uncertain of our ability to project positivity, as we wouldn't easily believe that we are significant in doing so, as significance held no value in our personal development.

It's time for the collective to heal; it's time to get value back as personal presence.

Most sincerely,
Athena Paloma
The Intuitive Rebel without a PhD

Printed in the United States
By Bookmasters